T0302005

Contemporary South Korean Economy: Challenges and Prospects

EAI Series on East Asia

ISSN: 2529-718X

Series Editors: WANG Gungwu
(East Asian Institute, National University of Singapore)

ZHENG Yongnian
(East Asian Institute, National University of Singapore)

About the Series

EAI Series on East Asia was initiated by the East Asian Institute (EAI) (http://www.eai.nus.edu.sg). EAI was set up in April 1997 as an autonomous research organisation under a statute of the National University of Singapore. The analyses in this series are by scholars who have spent years researching on their areas of interest in East Asia, primarily, China, Japan and South Korea, and in the realms of politics, economy, society and international relations.

Published:

The Rise of the Regulatory State in the Chinese Health-care System
by QIAN Jiwei

Contemporary South Korean Economy: Challenges and Prospects
by CHIANG Min-Hua

EAI Series on
East Asia

Contemporary South Korean Economy: Challenges and Prospects

CHIANG Min-Hua

East Asian Institute
National University of Singapore
Singapore

 World Scientific

NEW JERSEY · LONDON · SINGAPORE · BEIJING · SHANGHAI · HONG KONG · TAIPEI · CHENNAI · TOKYO

Published by

World Scientific Publishing Co. Pte. Ltd.
5 Toh Tuck Link, Singapore 596224
USA office: 27 Warren Street, Suite 401-402, Hackensack, NJ 07601
UK office: 57 Shelton Street, Covent Garden, London WC2H 9HE

Library of Congress Cataloging-in-Publication Data
Names: Chiang, Min-Hua, 1978–   author.
Title: Contemporary South Korean economy : challenges and prospects /
    by Min Hua Chiang, East Asian Institute, National University of Singapore.
Description: Hackensack, NJ : World Scientific Publishing Co. Pte. Ltd., [2017] |
    Series: EAI series on East Asia
Identifiers: LCCN 2017010607 | ISBN 9789813207233
Subjects: LCSH: Korea (South)--Economic conditions--21st century. |
    Economic development--Korea (South)--History--21st century. |
    Income distribution--Korea (South). | International economic relations.
Classification: LCC HC467.96 .C42725 2017 | DDC 330.95195--dc23
LC record available at https://lccn.loc.gov/2017010607

British Library Cataloguing-in-Publication Data
A catalogue record for this book is available from the British Library.

Desk Editor: Dong Lixi

Typeset by Stallion Press
Email: enquiries@stallionpress.com

Printed in Singapore

Contents

About the Author

Dr CHIANG Min-Hua is research fellow at the East Asian Institute (EAI), National University of Singapore. She obtained her PhD in economics from Université Pierre-Mendès-France, now part of Université Grenoble Alpes, in 2008 (avec la mention: Très honorable avec félicitations du jury). Before joining EAI in 2011, she held research positions at the Institute of International Relations, Chengchi University (2009), Taiwan External Trade Development Council (2009–2010) and Commerce Development Research Institute (2010–2011) in Taipei. Her research interests include Asia-Pacific regionalism, trade and investment, issues related to economic growth and development in East Asia.

Abbreviations

APEC	Asia-Pacific Economic Cooperation
BOK	Bank of Korea
EFTA	European Free Trade Association
FDI	Foreign direct investment
FSC	Financial Services Commission
FTA	Free trade agreement
GDP	Gross domestic product
HCI	Heavy and chemical industry
ICT	Information and communications technology
IPR	Intellectual property right
ITA	Information technology agreement
KORUS FTA	Republic of Korea-United States Free Trade Agreement
KRW	Korean Won
LCDs	Liquid crystal devices
M&A	Mergers and acquisitions
MERS	Middle East respiratory syndrome
NABO	National Assembly Budget Office
NAFTA	North America Free Trade Agreement
ODI	Outward direct investment
OECD	Organisation for Economic Cooperation and Development
OLED	Organic light-emitting diode
OPEC	Organisation of the Petroleum Exporting Countries

PRC	People's Republic of China
RCEP	Regional Comprehensive Economic Partnership
ROK	Republic of Korea
SMEs	Small and medium-sized enterprises
TFR	Total fertility rate
TPP	Trans-Pacific Partnership
TRIPS	Trade-related aspects of intellectual property rights
WTO	World Trade Organisation
WWII	World War II

Preface

South Korea's remarkable post-war economic development has often been lauded as a success story. From import-substitution in the 1950s to export expansion during the 1960s–1970s period, and further to the gradual economic liberalisation after the 1980s, Korea's economic development path has often been considered as a model for developing countries. Compared with the massive literature on South Korea's post-war development, its development after its successful post-war industrialisation was relatively less discussed. Hence, this book purports to provide an analytical review of South Korea's economic development in the two recent decades. In particular, the book aims to explore the main economic features and concerns after South Korea has achieved its post-war industrialisation. Several issues in contemporary Korean economy are selected for in-depth analyses in the different chapters of the book, including the changing drivers of economic growth, large business' importance to the economy, South Korea's free trade agreements (FTAs) with its most important trading partners, namely, the United States and China, growing income inequality and the ageing demography. Through the investigation of key development issues in the Korean economy today, its economic prospects and potential development challenges are further assessed and deliberated.

Although South Korea's economy was hit hard during the Asian financial crisis, its brilliant economic performance afterwards drew no less worldwide attention than during the Cold War era. Its economic advancement after the crisis has made it one of the major G-20 economies. Goldman Sachs investment bank had identified South Korea as one of the "Next 11" countries[1] and the MIST nations (Mexico, Indonesia, South Korea and Turkey) in 2005 and 2011 respectively, a positive appraisal of South Korea's economic growth potential. South Korea's economic achievement was highlighted further by the Korean government's announcement that the country has entered the exclusive "20-50 club" in 2012, with over US$20,000 of per capita national income and a population of more than 50 million. Currently only six countries (Japan, the United States, France, Italy, Germany and the UK) qualify for the "20–50" Club membership.

South Korea's economic recovery after the 1997–1998 turmoil has much to do with its chaebols' international business expansion, particularly in the information and communications technology (ICT) sectors. Today, Korea's ICT giants such as Samsung and LG are leading ICT branded products in the world. Beyond the ICT sectors, Korean chaebols have also made extensive international expansion in the shipbuilding, car making, entertainment, restaurants and retailing sectors over the last two decades. Chaebols' dominance in Korea's economy has however, squeezed the development of small and medium entreprises (SMEs). The strong opposition from society after several chaebols' involvement in the Park-Choi corruption case in 2016 has added uncertainty to chaebols' business domestically and internationally if the government were to break off close ties with chaebols in the future.

Indeed, economic development is not only about the quantitative aspects. A country's development is often accompanied by qualitative changes such as technological progress and structural changes in production and employment. In South Korea's case, behind the dazzling economic performance, the country has experienced dramatic structural changes that have brought about outstanding economic and social transformation. However, not every Korean rejoices to such changes. According to *OECD Economic Surveys in 2012*, 86% of South Koreans

---

[1] Next 11 countries include Bangladesh, Egypt, Indonesia, Iran, Mexico, Nigeria, Pakistan, the Philippines, South Korea, Turkey and Vietnam.

felt that economic benefits have not been fairly distributed, the highest percentage among 34 countries surveyed. The inadequate welfare spending, insufficient employment opportunities for domestic workers and unequal distribution of income plus the ageing demography have posed stumbling blocks to the country's sustainable development.

Despite its policy-oriented analysis, this book could inject new elements to the debate and discussion of conventional development theories. On one hand, the book shows the waning of the "developmental state" in South Korea today. With increasing globalisation, the state is less able to direct its economic development path as it had done before. Instead, state policies have to accommodate the globalisation trend. On the other hand, economic liberalisation may not necessarily mean that the economy will be fully operated by the "invisible hand". As Kalinowski argued in his article in 2009,[2] South Korea's market reform after the Asian financial crisis was a political negotiation process between the government, chaebols and other interest groups. The post-crisis liberalisation in South Korea is therefore a consequence of internal political fights responding to external environment changes. In terms of external economic relations, South Korea has signed many FTAs with other countries in recent years. FTAs are supposedly to benefit all based on a country's comparative advantages. In reality, however, the regulations and rules set by FTAs are often a result of a country's bargaining power. Political factors still play an important role in South Korea's domestic economy as well as its external economic relations.

This book is an extension of my *Background Briefs* with the East Asian Institute (EAI), written between 2013 and 2016. I am indebted to Professor Zheng Yongnian and Dr Sarah Tong of EAI for their helpful comments at the initial stage. I benefited from discussing Korean issues with Professor Choi Won-mog on his visit to the National University of Singapore and Dr KyuJin Shim of the Singapore

---

[2] T Kalinowski, "The Politics of Market Reforms: Korea's Path from Chaebol Republic to Market Democracy and Back", *Contemporary Politics*, vol. 15, no. 3, September 2009, pp. 287–304.

Management University. I would like to thank the editorial assistance of Ms Jessica Loon who brings this book to fruition. The academic environment at the institute has been very conducive for intellectual activities. The regular informal discussions and seminars at the institute have enlightened me on my research and broaden my horizon and understanding of this dynamic region as well as the global political economy. Throughout the book, "Korea", "South Korea" and Republic of Korea" (ROK) have been used interchangeably and refer to the same country unless otherwise specified. Finally, I bear sole responsibility for every issue covered and mistake found in this book.

Chapter 1

South Korea's Economy at a Crossroads

South Korea's phenomenal economic success post-World War II (WWII) has been widely hailed as another economic miracle after Japan's. In less than two decades after the war, South Korea had transformed from an agricultural nation to a major manufacturer in the world. The successful industrialisation from light to heavy industries had sustained the country's high economic growth rates for nearly four decades since the 1960s; the exceptions were the oil crisis and Asian financial crisis that dragged down its economic growth to negative rates in 1980 (−1.9%) and 1998 (−5.7%). The quicker gross domestic product (GDP) expansion than population growth rapidly augmented South Korea's GDP per capita from merely US$91.5 in 1961 to US$7,523 in 1991 and US$27,195 in 2015. The successful industrialisation also allowed manufacturing sectors to provide job opportunities for the mass labour released from the agricultural sectors, pulling tens of millions of people out of poverty. Despite the gradual relocation of manufacturing production to overseas countries since the 1990s, the unemployment rate continued to remain relatively low from 1990 to 2015 (between 2% and 4%) except for in 1998 and 1999.

The smooth economic development over the last few decades, however, is no shield for the problems and challenges that continue to plague South Korea's economy today. The continuous economic slowdown in recent years indicated that the long-term economic growth model based on exports has encountered difficulties. Not only does South Korea has to contend with the Japanese, its long-term rival, it now also has to face another emerging but equally if not more competitive economic powerhouse, the Chinese. The unclear export prospect has already led policymakers in Korea to remain dependent on extra government spending for maintaining its economic growth. Korea's heavy household and corporate debts are also the country's major weakness as a spike in interest rate or a sharp economic slowdown could lead to serious debt default that will further erode the government's financial strength.

This chapter aims to offer an overall evaluation of South Korea's macroeconomic performance and main policy response to the sluggish economy in recent years in a few significant areas: the main components of GDP growth and the resultant reasons behind the recent economic slowdown; the external trade development; the foreign direct investment (FDI) in South Korea and South Korean companies' expansion through outward direct investment (ODI); the piling South Korea's household and corporate debts; and the growth potential of Korea, both short-term and long-term.

Explaining South Korea's Economic Slowdown

South Korea's economy grew 2.6% in 2015, well below its projection of 3.9% at the beginning of the year, attributed largely to the weak exports and sluggish private consumption brought about by the spread of the Middle East respiratory syndrome (MERS) between May and July 2015. However, looking at Korea's economic growth in a wider timespan, the slower economic expansion had taken place a few years ago. Between 2010 and 2012, the sluggish economic growth was accompanied by shrinking activities in both manufacturing and services (Figure 1-1). In 2013, economic growth rebounded with a more significant recovery in manufacturing than in services. However, since the second quarter of 2014, manufacturing growth has fluctuated while services have been relatively stable. The deceleration of domestic manufacturing production is linked to Korea's slow growth in merchandise trade in the recent years. Korea's total trade improved very slightly from US$1,145 billion in 2011 to US$1,150 billion in 2014. In 2015,

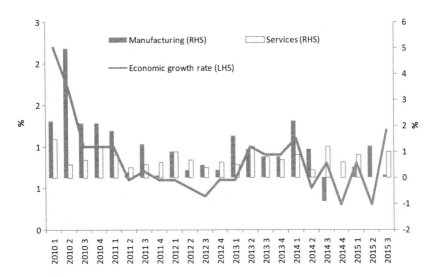

Figure 1-1   Growth Rate of South Korea's GDP by Sector 2010–2015
(Percentage change from previous quarter)

Source: Korea's Economic Statistics System, Bank of Korea, <http://ecos.bok.or.kr/> (accessed 11 December 2015).

exports and imports declined 8% and 17% respectively compared to that in the same period in 2014.

Several factors are behind South Korea's weak exports. First, China's increasing manufacturing strength may have reduced its reliance on importing intermediate goods from Korea. Indeed, China is no longer a low-end assembly location for South Korean manufacturers. Although intermediate goods continue to take a large portion of Korea's total exports to China, the percentages have been declining over the last decade. Second, South Korea's declining manufacturing investment in China might have reduced China-based Korean firms' import of inter-mediate goods from home companies in South Korea. Third, Korea's poor export performance is also related to the weaker Japanese yen. Korean Won (KRW) dipped from 13.8 won to 1 Japanese yen in the third quarter of 2010 to 9.7 won in the third quarter of 2015. During this period, the quarterly export growth rates had been waning as shown in Figure 1-2. Given the strong competition between Korean

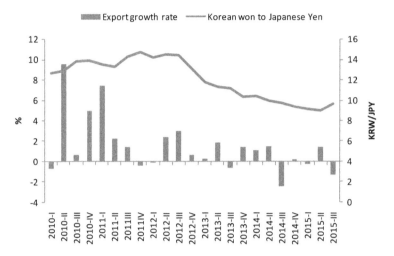

Figure 1-2   Korean Export Growth Rate and Korean Won's Exchange Rate to Japanese Yen 2010–2015

Source: CEIC.

and Japanese manufacturers in the global market, especially in automobile, machinery and electronic sectors, yen's depreciation has eroded the competitiveness of Korean products. About 70% of respondents surveyed in 2015 by Korea International Trade Association claimed that a weaker yen is wiping out their export business.[1] The Bank of Korea (BOK) has limited tools to counterbalance the impact of a weaker yen despite its vast dollar reserves. Selling Korean won against US dollar and yen to depreciate KRW will impact on Korea's business in the import of raw materials. Moreover, a weaker won could discourage foreign investors in the stock and bond market, thus destabilising the South Korean financial market.

In the face of weak exports, domestic consumption and investment became vital for supporting the country's economic growth. The government expected the recovery of the housing market to contribute to

---

[1] Tae Moonyoung, "Korea Exporters Turn Screws on BOK to Sell Won as Yen Sinks", *Bloomberg*, 28 May 2015, <http://www.bloomberg.com/news/articles/2015-05-28/korean-exporters-turn-screws-on-bok-to-weaken-won-as-yen-sinks> (accessed 26 October 2015).

the growth in private consumption. However, the accumulated household debt following rising housing prices might have restrained the growth in private consumption. Indeed, the key for promoting private consumption shall come from the steady growth in salary. The slow wage growth is a constraint on people's propensity to consume. Over the last decade, the average monthly income of households with more than two persons increased by less than 2% annually. The most critical is the enlarging income gap. The gap between the average monthly incomes of the top 10% and the bottom 10% widened from 5.59 million won (US$4,847) in 2004 to 8.63 million won (US$7,483) in 2014.[2]Although the figure in 2015 showed that unemployment rate remained low (3.2%), 51% of the employed was irregular workers (including temporary, daily and self-employed unpaid family workers).[3] As irregular workers' salary is lower and less stable compared to that of regular workers, their financial situation is vulnerable to an economic slowdown.

Even with the growing household debts, the government continued with its broad policy of stimulating economic growth by easing mortgage restrictions and cutting interest rates to 1.5% in June 2015.[4] In August 2015, the government further announced a cut in consumption tax to spur private consumption. Excise taxes levied on cars, large household appliances and certain health food supplements had been reduced by 30% until the end of 2015.[5]

Private investment from corporates is another essential element in GDP growth. Nonetheless, the feeble exports had discouraged private

---

[2]"Structural Approach Needed to Boost Domestic Consumption", *The Korea Herald*, 26 October 2015, <http://www.koreaherald.com/view.php?ud=20151026001078 > (accessed 16 November 2015).

[3]"Economically Active Population Survey in October 2015", Statistics Korea.

[4]"S. Korea Takes Steps to Better Manage Growing Household Debt", Reuters, 22 July 2015, <http://www.reuters.com/article/2015/07/21/southkorea-economy-debt-idUSL3N1012CO20150721> (accessed 23 October 2015).

[5]"Korea to Reduce Consumption Taxes to Boost Economy", *The Korea Herald*, 26 August 2015, <http://www.koreaherald.com/view.php?ud=20150826001156> (accessed 26 October 2015).

sectors' short-term investment in manufacturing goods for exports. The government's investment was therefore important at the time when both private consumption and investment were fragile. In March 2015, Korea's Ministry of Finance announced a budget of three trillion won (US$2.6 billion) for fiscal expenditure in the first half of the year.[6] In July, it announced another fiscal stimulus package of 22 trillion won (US$19.6 billion) to spur anaemic growth. This stimulus package was mostly to be funded by issuing government debt and various state funds with a focus on financing MERS-hit businesses, reinforcing quarantine facilities and creating more jobs.[7] In the face of a potential contraction in exports, the South Korean government planned to spend 386.7 trillion won (US$320 billion) in 2016, an increase of two trillion won (US$14 billion) from 384.7 trillion won (US$334 billion) in 2015 to maintain the country's growth. Thirty-two per cent of the budget in 2016 would go to welfare programmes, followed by 16% to public administration, 14% to education and 10% to military defence.[8] The growing budget is expected to widen the fiscal deficit to 37 trillion won (US$32 billion), representing 2.3% of Korea's GDP in 2016, the highest since 2009. The wider fiscal deficit was also expected to push the country's sovereign debt to a record high of 40.1% of its GDP in 2016, a rate which was still much lower than the Organisation for Economic Co-operation and Development (OECD) countries' average of 114.6% in 2015.[9]

---

[6]"Boosting the Economy", *The Korea Herald*, 23 March 2015, <http://www.koreaherald.com/ view.php?ud=20150323000512> (accessed 26 October 2015).

[7]Jun Kwanwoo, "South Korea Announces $20B Fiscal Stimulus to Spur Economy", *The Wall Street Journal*, 2 July 2015, <http://www.wsj.com/articles/SB10622146353 0718048678045810848222203731598> (accessed 26 October 2015).

[8]Cynthia Kim, "South Korea Plans Record 2016 Budget as Park Seek Growth", *Bloomberg*, 8 September 2015, <http://www. bloomberg.com/news/articles/ 2015-09-08/south-korea-plans-record-budget-for-2016-as-park-seeks-growth> (17 November 2015).

[9]Nam In-Soo "South Korea Fiscal Deficit Seen at Seven-Year High in 2016", *Wall Street Journal*, 8 September 2015.

From a positive point of view, given South Korea's relatively low government debt to GDP ratio compared to other OECD countries, the higher government expenditure is less likely to erode its financial soundness in the near term. However, the stimulus policy may not be sustainable if exports continue to fall. The decreasing exports mean that Korean firms are making less money and producing less tax revenues. As a consequence, the government will have less capacity to finance the extra spending for boosting the economy.

Growing Trade Surplus and Korea's FTAs Expansion

Trade expansion has facilitated South Korea's economic development over the last few decades. Being a resource poor country, South Korea has to rely on importing energy resources for domestic production. The domestically made products also need access to foreign markets for South Korea's economy to continue its upward climb. The substantial commercial exchanges with other countries have made South Korea an important global trader. According to the World Trade Organisation (WTO), South Korea was the seventh largest exporter and ninth largest importer in the world in 2013.[10]

Despite its considerable exports, South Korea's trade balance was a constant deficit from 1960 to 1985 for the greater import that it had registered. The country enjoyed a surplus in 1986 only to slide into deficit again from 1990 to 1997. The turning point was in 1998; except for 2008 South Korea has run trade surplus continuously since.[11] As exhibited in Figure 1-3, South Korea's overall merchandise trade showed clear growth after plunging in 2008 and progressing slowly from 2011 to 2012. With growing maturity, South Korean exports have steadily gained their foothold in overseas markets, registering a trade balance from US$28 billion in 2012 to US$47 billion in 2014. In 2015, the trade balance reached a record high of US$73 billion. The clear growth in trade surplus in 2015 was mainly due to lower oil prices

---

[10] *International Trade Statistics 2014*, World Trade Organisation, p. 26.
[11] Data source: CEIC.

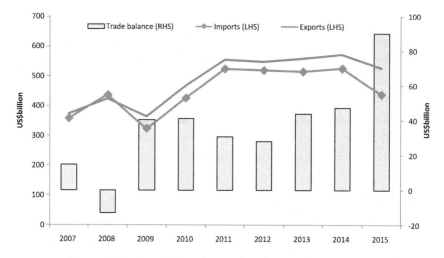

Figure 1-3 South Korea's Merchandise Trade 2007–2015

Source: CEIC and World Trade Atlas.

in the international market, allowing major industries that demanded large imports of oil and gas, such as shipbuilding, to have cheap imports of oil and mineral fuel.

China is the largest export destination for South Korea, accounting for 26% of total Korean exports in 2015. With the inclusion of Hong Kong, China's weight in Korea's exports would be 32%. Ten countries in Association of Southeast Asian Nations (ASEAN) were the second largest export destination (14%), followed by the United States (13%), the European Union (EU) (9%) and south and central America (6%) (Figure 1-4). Unlike exports of mainly vehicles and boats to the United States and the EU, half of Korea's exports to China are electrical machinery and machinery. China, including Hong Kong is also Korea's most important source of imports, constituting 21% of its imports in 2015. The main import items from China included the final ICT products such as smartphones, computers, tablets and so on, accounting for 13% of total imports from China. Although China has been gradually changing from a labour-intensive assembly location to a more technology-intensive production site, South Korea continued to

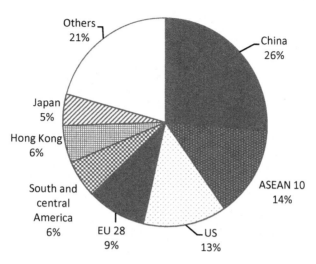

Figure 1-4   South Korea's Major Export Destinations in 2015
Source: World Trade Atlas.

rely on exporting intermediate goods to China for its economic survival and on importing final goods after assembling in China. While this may indicate that South Korea still possesses comparative advantages in certain high technology and high capital intensive products vis-à-vis China, its slowing economy following declining exports to China implies that the technology gap between the two countries could be narrowing. Beyond importing ICT final products from China, South Korea also depends on importing foreign energy resources. Its import of oil chiefly from the Organisation of the Petroleum Exporting Countries (OPEC) was a significant share of 15% of its imports, followed by the EU's 13%, Japan's 11%, ASEAN-10's 10% and the United States' 10% (Figure 1-5).

South Korea's trade relations with 10 countries in ASEAN are similar to its trade relations with China. The investment-driven trade has accounted for a large portion of South Korea-ASEAN total trade. South Korea supplied intermediate goods to ASEAN chiefly for its own manufacturing bases in these countries. In 2015, 40% of Korea's exports to and 32% of its imports from ASEAN were machinery and

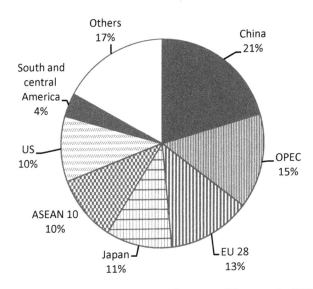

Figure 1-5   South Korea's Main Sources of Imports in 2015

Source: World Trade Atlas.

electrical machinery.[12] As many ASEAN countries are rich in natural resources, they are also South Korea's chief import source for mineral fuels.

The gradual trade liberalisation since the 1980s has boosted South Korea's total trade volumes. The greater commitment to international trade rules and principles after joining WTO in 1995 further encouraged it to phase in agreed tariff reduction and other non-tariff barriers. Nonetheless, South Korea was still reputed to be a difficult market with excessive bureaucracy, high imposts on many imports and perceived consumer and official bias against imported goods during the 1990s. [13]

South Korea's launch of extensive FTA network since the early 2000s to gain greater access to foreign markets has further promoted

---

[12] Data source: World Trade Atlas.

[13] *Korea Rebuilds: From Crisis to Opportunity*, East Asia Analytical Unit, Department of Foreign Affairs and Trade, Australia, 1999, p. 53.

the country's external trade. The network is especially important for South Korea to explore new avenues to sustain its export-led growth when China's economy is on the downward trend in recent years. Indeed, South Korea's growth in trade surplus since 2009 has been accompanied by the smooth expansion of its FTAs. Korea-US FTA was signed in June 2007 and has been effective since 2012. Total surplus with the United States progressed from US$9.4 billion in 2010 to US$25 billion in 2014.[14] Korea-EU FTA took effect from July 2011 with different results. Trade balance with the EU developed from a surplus of US$15 billion in 2010 to a deficit of US$1 billion in 2014. Korea's imports of food and heavy industrial goods, such as aircraft and vehicles from the EU, have registered significant growth after the implementation of the bilateral FTA.[15] South Korea's FTA with China on 1 June 2015 took effect in December of the same year. FTAs with other economies, such as Chile, Singapore, European Free Trade Association (EFTA),[16] ASEAN, India and Peru, have entered into force. FTAs with Turkey and Colombia have also been concluded, while FTAs with Canada, Mexico, Australia, New Zealand, Vietnam and Indonesia are under negotiation.[17] At the multilateral level, South Korea is part of Regional Comprehensive Economic Partnership (RCEP) but not a member of Trans-Pacific Partnership (TPP). Owing to its extensive FTAs, the economic benefits of joining the TPP are considered less imperative by Korean officials. Korea's TPP delay may also be a result of its intention to finalise the FTA with China first.[18]

---

[14] Data source: CEIC.

[15] Data source: World Trade Atlas.

[16] EFTA includes Iceland, Norway, Liechtenstein and Switzerland.

[17] "FTA Status of ROK", Ministry of Foreign Affairs, Republic of Korea, <http://www.mofa.go.kr/ ENG/policy/fta/status/overview/index.jsp?menu=m_20_80_10> (accessed 29 October 2015).

[18] Jessica J Lee, "The Truth about South Korea's TPP Shift", *The Diplomat*, 23 October 2015, <http://thediplomat.com/2015/10/the-truth-about-south-koreas-tpp-shift/> (accessed 29 October 2015).

Quick Growth in Outward Investment While Inward FDI Progresses Slowly

Unlike other Asian dragons, the Korean government did not implement inward FDI promotion policy for its post-war industrialisation. Hence, South Korea's foreign capital was mostly short-term foreign borrowing, making it vulnerable to the Asian financial crisis in 1997. After the crisis, the government has begun to recognise the country's structural weakness and revised the policy to encourage FDI. The Kim Dae-jung government regarded FDI as essential to recapitalising and restructuring financial institutions. In the long run, FDI was considered beneficial for the country's development as it could increase domestic business competition, upgrade technologies and change the corporate culture.[19]

The FDI promotion policy after the Asian financial crisis was a success. Inward FDI increased rapidly from US$3 billion in 1996 to US$16 billion in 1999. After 2000 however, progress has been slow, increasing from US$15 billion in 2000 to nearly US$21 billion in 2015 (Figure 1-6). The Korean government has continued to promote FDI from advanced countries for the high technology and employment it brings in compensation for the loss of jobs at home subsequent to the relocation of factories abroad. The improvement in the investment environment in South Korea explained the growing FDI. According to the Ease of Doing Business Rank (out of 189 economies), Korea's ranking progressed from 23rd in 2007 to fourth in 2016, only behind Singapore, New Zealand and Denmark.[20]

As shown in Figure 1-7, the United States is the most important investor in South Korea, accounting for 22% of total inward FDI in 2015, followed by the EU (14%), China (11%) and Japan (9%). Although the United Sates remained the leading foreign investor in South Korea, the investment shares from the United States had witnessed

---

[19] *Korea Rebuilds: From Crisis to Opportunity*, East Asia Analytical Unit, Department of Foreign Affairs and Trade, Australia, 1999, p. 79.

[20] "Doing Business", World Bank Group, <http://www.doingbusiness.org/rankings> (accessed 3 November 2015).

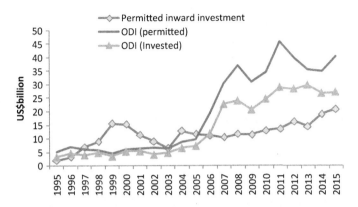

Figure 1-6   South Korea's Inward and Outward Investment 1995–2015

Source: CEIC.

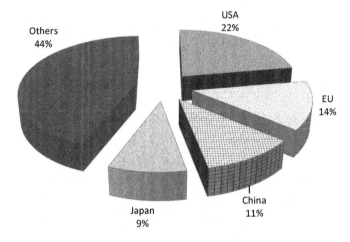

Figure 1-7   South Korea's FDI by Country in 2015

Source: CEIC.

a significant drop over the past few years. For example, the United States accounted for 49% of Korea's total FDI in 2002. Similarly Japan also took a large share (54%) in 2008. In the last few years, however, there was an obvious increase of FDI from China, a result of China's overwhelming ODI in recent years. South Korea is an attractive destination for China's growing outward investment wave.

In terms of FDI by sectors, since 2000, service sectors have become dominant in Korea's FDI. In 2015, services accounted for 67% of total FDI. Chinese Anbang Insurance Group's US$1 billion buyout of Korea's Tong Yang Life Insurance led robust FDI growth in 2015.[21] Looking into the future, China's investment in Korea is likely to rise further as the Chinese government is encouraging Chinese companies to expand their business abroad. The implementation of China-Korea FTA is also expected to further boost investment and economic cooperation between the two countries.

Unlike the inward FDI which has been largely deregulated after 1997, South Korea began to relax the rules for ODI as early as in 1987. During the initial ODI liberalisation, the bulk of ODI centred on natural resource investment projects to secure stable resource supply to the country. Another motivation for ODI was to avoid the host country's import barriers.[22] Over the last few decades, the development of ODI has varied in line with domestic industrial changes, from light industries to ICT sectors. Production cost, including labour cost and land prices in host countries, has remained the primary consideration for investment.

As indicated in Figure 1-6, South Korea's ODI developed relatively slowly during the 1995 and 2005 period compared to its inward FDI. The permitted ODI ranged between US$4.7 billion and US$9.8 billion during the same period. However, South Korea's permitted ODI has shown robust growth, surpassing its inward FDI since 2006. It peaked at US$46 billion in 2011 and declined slightly to US$40 billion in 2015. Similar growth pattern can be found in Korea's invested ODI (Figure 1-6). The quick development of ODI has been attributed to its investment surge in China since 2002. According to Korea's Eximbank, between 2002 and 2007, 24%-39% of Korea's invested ODI was in China. The geographic proximity and cheap labour force

---

[21] "Foreign Investment in Korea Is on the Rise", *Korea Joongang Daily*, 5 October 2015, <http://koreajoongangdaily.joins.com/news/article/Article.aspx?aid=3009891> (accessed 2 November 2015).

[22] *Korea Rebuilds: From Crisis to Opportunity*, p. 93.

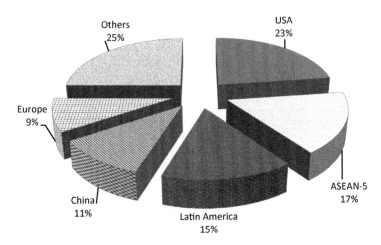

Figure 1-8   South Korea's Invested ODI by Country in 2015

Source: CEIC.

made China an attractive manufacturing site for Korean manufacturers. However, China's share in South Korea's ODI has decreased after 2008. In 2015, China accounted for only 11% of Korea's total invested ODI (Figure 1-8). The declining investment share in China took place when the investment shares in five major countries in ASEAN, namely, Malaysia, Vietnam, Thailand, Indonesia and Singapore (ASEAN-5) and Latin America have expanded smoothly. Both regions accounted for a respective 17% and 15% of total Korea ODI in 2015. As investments in manufacturing continued to increase over the last decade, the greater investment share in ASEAN-5 and Latin America implied that the investment could be at the expense of China's share.

The FTA with the United States might have boosted Korean ODI to the country. A year before Republic of Korea-United States Free Trade Agreement (KORUS FTA) took effect, Korea's total invested ODI share in the United States recorded significant growth to 25% in 2011, from 14% in the previous year. In 2015, America was Korea's largest ODI destination, accounting for 23% of Korea's total invested ODI. In comparison, the effect on ODI from the FTA with Europe is less noteworthy. ODI share in Europe plunged to 9% in 2015 from 26% in 2009. In terms of ODI by sector, mining, financial services and construction have displayed clear growth over the last decade. In 2015, 33% of Korea's ODI was in manufacturing, followed by mining (15%), financial services (17%), wholesale and retail (11%), real estate (6%) and construction (6%).[23]

Growing Debts Sap Korea's Growth Potential

In 2014, Korea's total debt to GDP ratio was 227%, including 38% of government debt, 105% of corporate debt and 84% of household debt. Although this ratio was higher than it was in 2007 (Figure 1-9), it was not particularly high vis-a-vis other countries (Table 1-1).

In terms of government debt to GDP ratio, it was especially low compared to most of the developing and developed countries. The Park administration hence believed that Korea would be able to bear higher government debt. Opposition parties thought otherwise, citing the ageing population and the large fund needed for the Korean reunification.[24]While government debt to GDP ratio is lower than that of many countries, household debt is higher than the average ratio (30%) of emerging countries and major developed countries, such as the United States (78%), Japan (66%), France (56%) and Germany (54%) (Table 1-1). After the Asian financial crisis, the high commodity price level set by the government, the widespread use of credit card to boost economic growth, the low interest policy that induced credit creation and the Korean financial institutions' shift of target customers from companies to individuals had contributed to the rapid household debt.[25] The housing market boom in the recent

---

[23]Data source: CEIC.

[24]"Korean Gov't Debt Exceeds 115 Percent of National GDP", *Business Korea*, 17 October 2014, <http://www.businesskorea.co.kr/english/news/politics/6853-government-debt-korean-govt-debt-exceeds-11 5-percent-national-gdp> (accessed 3 November 2015).

[25]Kim Jongsung, "The Impact of Household Debt on Korea's Economy and Society", 18 June 2013, Academic paper series, Korea Economic Institute of America, <http://www.keia.org/publication/impact-household-debt-koreas-economy-and-society> (accessed 4 November 2015).

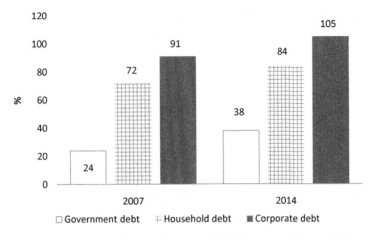

Figure 1-9   South Korea's Debt to GDP Ratio in 2007 and 2014

Source: *BIS Quarterly Review*, Bank for International Settlements, September 2015, p. 84.

TABLE 1-1   Debt to GDP Ratio in 2014, Selected Economies

Unit: %

	Government Debt	Household Debt	Corporate Debt	Total Debt
Advanced economies	110	73	81	265
Australia	35	119	77	230
Canada	70	93	104	267
France	109	56	124	288
Germany	82	54	54	191
Italy	151	43	78	272
Japan	222	66	105	393
UK	107	87	77	271
US	92	78	69	239
Emerging market economies	44	30	94	167
Brazil	43	6	9	58
China	41	36	157	235
Hong Kong	5	66	217	287
India	66	9	50	125
Korea	38	84	105	227
Malaysia	53	69	64	186
Singapore	99	61	82	242

Source: *BIS Quarterly Review*, Bank for International Settlements, September 2015, p. 84.

years further pushed up household debts mostly from housing loans. Up to June 2015, mortgage loans accounted for 44% of total household loans in all financial institutions.[26] Non-bank financial institutions, which are less strictly regulated by the government than banks, took an important share in mortgages. At the end of Q1 2016, household loans made by banks totalled 569.3 trillion won (US$0.48 trillion), almost equalling the 589.1 trillion won (US$0.5 trillion) made by non-bank financial institutions.[27] Although there is a concern that rising housing price could add on to household debt, Minister of Strategy and Finance Choi Kyung-hwan argued that the debt is mostly incurred by those with high income and a low default rate.[28] To counterbalance the worries about growing household debt, the government encouraged companies to increase workers' income and imposes a 10% tax penalty on excessive corporate cash reserves while offering tax breaks for companies using such cash holding to increase wages, investment and dividends.[29]

Korea has a relatively higher ratio of corporate debt to GDP than the average ratio in both advanced and emerging market economies except for China, Hong Kong and France (Table 1-1). In 2014, 81% of Korea's corporate debt came from private companies while 19% was by public corporations.[30] The high corporate debt could spell operational problems for corporate companies especially during the economic recession period. According to a survey released by the BOK in October 2015, 32% of the companies surveyed were not financially sound. Another survey indicated that 10% of the top 500 companies

---

[26] "Household Credits in Q2 2015", August 2015, Economic Statistics Department, Bank of Korea.

[27] *Financial Stability Report*, June 2016, p. 28.

[28] Song June-a, "South Korea Households Pile up Debt", *Financial Times*, 5 January 2015.

[29] Song Jung-a, "South Korean Households Pile up Debt".

[30] "S. Korea's Ratio of Corporate Debt to GDP High: Report", *Yonhap News*, 20 April 2015, <http://english.yonhapnews.co.kr/business/2015/04/20/82/0502000000AEN20150420001400320F.html> (accessed 3 November 2015).

in Korea were financially insolvent in 2014.[31] Most financially insolvent Korean companies borrowed from state-run banks or from financial institutions backed by the government. With the continued economic slowdown and more insolvent companies, it could probably be a risk to state-run banks as well as the government's fiscal strength.

Despite the concerns about high household and corporate debts to economic stability, some pointed out that a debt-triggered financial crisis is unlikely with Korea's large current account surplus (US$9.8 billion in September 2015) and foreign exchange reserves (US$369.6 billion in October 2015, making South Korea the seventh largest foreign exchange reserve holder in the world).[32] Optimists also believed that Korean banks' interest rate hike in the future would reduce borrowing, hence leading to a decline in debt.[33] Nevertheless, the decrease in borrowing will also result in a reduction in consumption and investment, the two essential elements for economic growth.

Conclusion

As discussed in the previous sections, South Korea's export sectors have encountered great difficulties in recent years. The soft demand from the main consumption market in the West, China's transformation towards more consumption-based economy, growing competition from Chinese manufacturers and Japanese yen's depreciation are main reasons for South Korea's declining exports.

The greater linkage with other countries through free trade and investment relaxation is considered important for sustaining South

---

[31] "Taking on Korea's Zombie Companies", *Korea Joongang Daily*, 3 November 2015, <http://koreajoongangdaily.joins.com/news/article/article.aspx?aid=3011063&cloc=joongangdaily%7Chome%7Cnewslist2> (accessed 16 November 2015).

[32] "Pulled Back In", *The Economist*, 14 November 2015, p. 24.

[33] Kim Boram, "Mounting Household Debt Poses Major Threat to S. Korea: Former Moody's Analyst", *Yonhap News Agency*, 17 November 2015, <http://english.yonhapnews.co.kr/news/2015/11/17/0200000000AEN20151117002400320.html> (accessed 25 November 2015).

Korea's economic development. Although South Korea has successfully secured a number of FTAs, notably with the United States, the EU and China, its trade structure based on regional production network remains relatively unchanged. South Korea's external trade is still promoted by exporting intermediate goods to developing countries while importing raw materials and energy resources from the Middle East or Southeast Asian countries. In the long run, the favourable terms that Korea enjoys under FTAs could dissipate if more countries are involved in the global free trade network.

Over the past two decades, Korean companies have successfully expanded and capitalised on their economies of scale by taking advantage of China's and other developing countries' less expensive labour force via ODI. As South Korea is moving towards an innovation-driven economy, FDI from advanced countries is considered important for acquiring foreign technology and providing greater high value-added job opportunities at home. Nonetheless, the inward FDI has progressed slowly over the past few years. Although both the United States and the EU remained South Korea's main source of FDI, the inward FDI from China has shown robust growth recently.

To minimise the potential impact from the falling exports, the South Korean government has launched several rounds of stimulus policies. Promoting the economy through extra government spending is necessary during the downward trend of the economic cycle. Despite its growing government debt concerns, South Korea's huge current account surplus and foreign exchange reserves are the country's buffer to any debt-triggered financial crisis. However, this is not to encourage more debt to sustain its economy. It could effectively prevent the economy from the deep recession in the short term. If exports continue their downward turn, the falling tax revenues will invalidate the stimulus policy, making it a short-term solution. The key to sustainable development is therefore to build sound export sectors in both manufacturing and services.

The most worrying issue in Korean economy is probably the threat to its financial stability brought about by its household and corporate debts. After being negatively impacted by the Asian financial crisis, both the Korean government and Korea watchers have paid much attention to the potential volatility of its financial debts. US interest rate hike raises concern about the possibility of large outflow of capital that could destabilise Korea financially. Past experiences have indicated the vulnerability of Korea's financial market to changes in the external environment. Between 2004 and 2006 when the United States' central bank raised its interest rate, it resulted in an outflow of 20 trillion won (US$17.5 billion).[34] Moreover, any corresponding increase in interest rate on its part will add more burden especially to low-income households in their housing loan repayment. Private domestic consumption will be further constrained as a result. Corporate debt is another unstable factor in the financial market. The collapse of some companies without strong financial backing could result in unemployment and impact on investment and private consumption. Although Korea's Financial Services Commission (FSC) had announced a plan to identify and clean up zombie companies in 2015, the scepticism about policy effectiveness remains.

From a positive point of view, the negative effect of US interest rate hike may not be significant given China's economic slowdown and potential impact on US exports; the Fed would implement a slight and gradual increase in response.[35] The recent interest rate hike by 0.25% in December 2015 was reflective of Fed's cautious move.

In the long run, Korea's economy will be facing the following challenges. First is the demographic change. Among 224 countries in the world in 2015, South Korea's fertility rate ranked 220.[36] Korean official estimates also show that its working age population is expected to

---

[34] Choi Sung-jin, "Korea Most Vulnerable to Emerging Economies' Crisis", *The Korea Times*, 13 November 2015, <http://www.koreatimes.co.kr/www/news/nation/2015/11/116_190906.html> (accessed 17 November 2015).

[35] "Pulled Back In", *The Economist*.

[36] "Total Fertility Rate", The World Factbook, <https://www.cia.gov/library/publications/the-world-factbook/rankorder/2127rank.html> (accessed 5 December 2015).

decrease from 37 million in 2016 to 33 million in 2030 and 29 million in 2040.[37] Second, despite President Park's pledge to narrow the income gap, the uncertain economic prospects have forced the Park administration to continue with its pro-large companies policies. Income inequality and economic injustice are likely to continue to be a concern. Third, if a unified Korea comes to fruition, it would drain South Korea's economy of an estimated US$500 billion to restore North Korea's economy. The reunification process will not only weaken South Korea's public finances but also put a downward pressure on the won.

In sum, South Korea's economy is now at a crossroads. The traditional approach that supported its economic growth through exporting intermediate goods to China during the last two decades can no longer effectively promote South Korea's economic growth. The country needs to look for new alternatives if it is to continue its upward climb. The fiscal stimulus policy is imperative during the time when the economy is adjusting towards more high value-added production and services. In the long run, South Korea will have to stand out in terms of advanced technology, strong innovation capacity, high quality services and irreplaceable position in the regional economic network. Creating a free competition environment will be key to South Korea's next phase in growth. Nonetheless, liberalising the economy to overseas competitors could benefit the most competitive industries while endangering the weaker ones. The government will have to develop a mechanism to support sectors disadvantaged by the liberalisation.

---

[37] "Demographic Challenges Undermine Korea's Growth Potential", *The Korea Herald*, 29 November 2015, <http://www.koreaherald.com/view.php?ud=20151129000386> (accessed 5 December 2015).

Chapter 2

Chaebol's Role in South Korea's Economic Development

With the government's strong support, chaebols'[1] importance in South Korea's economy has grown quickly since the 1960s. The country has also become a key manufacturer in both heavy industry and high technology sectors in the world thanks to chaebols' business success. However, South Korea's economic turmoil after the Asian financial crisis exposed the weakness of its growth model based on government-backed chaebols. Some chaebol affiliates either went bankrupt or were sold to foreign investors after the post-crisis reforms, while some have continued to develop with steady net profit growth. After the 2008–2009 global financial crisis, wealth has noticeably gone to a few surviving chaebols, which, despite their immense business success, employ only a small percentage of the local working population. Notably, the pro-chaebols economic policies after the crisis benefited only this small group of people at the expense of a large number of workers in the small and medium-sized enterprises (SMEs).

---

[1] A chaebol refers to a business organisation comprising a multiple number of monopolistic or oligopolistic large firms which diversify into various markets or industries and are substantially owned and managed by a specific individual, his or her family, or a small number of people under his or her control. Lee Jae Hyung, *Policy Issues of Corporate Governance in Korean Chaebols: Lessons from the Japanese Experiences*, Korea Development Institute, December 2003.

This chapter provides an analytical review of Korean chaebols' development and their changing importance in South Korea's economy over the last few decades. The first section provides a historical background to chaebols' development after WWII and the second section shows chaebols' development post-Asian financial crisis reform. The third section gives an overview of top chaebols' business expansion after the global financial crisis, while the fourth section examines how the government promotes economic growth through their cooperation with chaebols. The fifth section discusses the impact of government-chaebol close ties on SMEs' development in South Korea. Finally, South Korea's chaebol-dominated economic outlook is summarised at the end of the chapter.

Fostering Chaebols to Industrialise South Korea

Korean chaebols' development began as early as in the 1950s. Several selected companies, which were either members or relatives of Rhee Syngman's ruling party members, benefited from purchasing former Japanese colonial government-owned properties at discounted prices, acquiring ownership of commercial banks and accessing imported goods financed by US aid. The overvaluation of Korean Won (KRW) to maximise arbitrage opportunities for certain domestic firms had discouraged exports. As a result, Rhee's policy turned the trading nation into a nearly aid-dependent economy.[2] In the 1950s and early 1960s, South Korea's economy was still lagging behind the North's in terms of per capita income, industrial production and technological level.[3]

---

[2] Lim Wonhyuk, "The Emergence of the Chaebol and the Origins of the Chaebol Problem", in Stephan Haggard, Lim Wonhyuk and Kim Euysung, *Economic Crisis and Corporate Restructuring in Korea*, Cambridge, Cambridge University Press, 2003, pp. 42–43.

[3] Lee Moosung and Shim Jae-Seung, "The Distorted Relationship between Chaebols and Korean Government: A historical overview from 1945 to 1996", *Current Politics and Economics of Northern and Western Asia*, vol. 22, no. 2, pp. 193–211.

A student protest in April 1960 put an end to the Rhee government. A new democratic government took office in August 1960 but failed to deal with problems inherited from the previous government, including economic mismanagement, corruption and social instability. In 1961, Park Chung-hee, a military general seized power through a coup. Unlike Rhee's government, a military government led by Park adopted drastic measures to promote exports and divert economic dependence from the United States. The government provided many incentives, such as preferential banking loans and induced foreign capital to private firms to spur their production capacity for exports. These measures led to an upswing of labour-intensive manufactured exports that bolstered South Korea's economic growth in the 1960s (Figure 2-1). Large companies were the main beneficiaries of this upsurge. Compared with other small firms, large companies were in a much better position as they could capitalise on the economies of scale of their production. The government also favoured a handful of large firms over a large number of small firms given the convenience of cooperating with a few business leaders.[4]

The Park government's promotion of heavy and chemical industry (HCI) in the 1970s further strengthened the government's coalition with large companies at the expense of smaller firms. Only a few selected large companies in HCI which enjoyed economies of scale received extremely generous government support. The government injected massive financial resources into these chaebols to launch national investment projects and took the responsibility for their success or failure.[5] The chaebol-led HCI development strategy was a success as evidenced by the higher economic growth rates (9.4%) compared to that a decade before. Since the 1980s, other high technology and high capital intensive industries such as semiconductors

---

[4] Lee Moosung and Shim Jae-Seung, "The Distorted Relationship between Chaebols and Korean Government", pp. 198-199.
[5] Lim Wonhyuk, "The Emergence of the Chaebol and the Origins of the Chaebol Problem", pp. 47-48.

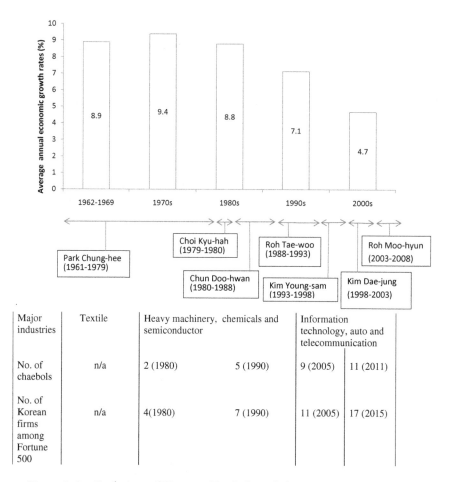

Figure 2-1   Evolution of Korean Chaebols and the Economy 1962–2010

Source: International Monetary Fund, World Economic Outlook Database, October 2015; Alice H Amsden, *Asia's Next Giant: South Korea and Late Industrialization*, 1989, Oxford University Press, Oxford and New York, p. 57; "Chaebol Structure", Key to Way Inc., <http://www.thekeytoway.com/demand_structure.php> (accessed 15 February 2016).

and ICT sectors were gradually developed and became new growth engines of South Korea's economy. Chaebols' business extension to other manufacturing sectors continued to receive government's strong support.

Due to concerns that the collapse of chaebols would seriously destabi-lise state-owned financial institutions with huge loans to chaebols, the government had to guarantee these financial loans in order to maintain the country's economic stability. Chaebols took advantage of this guaran-tee and made excessive investment in a variety of sectors to expand their business. With easy access to subsidised credit, low labour cost and pro-tected domestic market from foreign competition, chaebols flourished in terms of numbers and size. The number of chaebols increased from merely two in 1980 to five in 1990, nine in 2005 and 11 in 2011. They gradually evolved into conglomerate groups controlling not only manufacturing sectors but also retailing, construction and non-bank financial sectors, thus strengthening their dominance in Korea's economy.[6] Nevertheless, chaebols' increasing importance in the economy has challenged the gov-ernment's dominant role in directing the economic development path. From the mid-1980s, several administrations had introduced policies to restrain chaebols' power expansion but without much success.[7] It was until the Asian financial crisis that several chaebols suffered great losses that their business structure and excessive investment were reviewed.

The government-chaebol risk-sharing partnership that created South Korea's post-war economic miracle was hit hard during the Asian financial crisis. The country was nearly insolvent due to the excessive foreign debt. The economic crisis also triggered a social crisis, with the unemployed more than doubled from 556,500 in 1997 to 1,463,400 in 1998.[8] Although the initial trigger for the crisis was from the Southeast Asian slumping currencies, Korean chaebols' heavy exposure to foreign borrowing and investments, coupled with weak financial control and poor corporate governance, had exposed Korea's structural weakness. Foreign investors soon lost their confidence in South Korea

---

[6] *Korea Rebuilds: From Crisis to Opportunities,* East Asian Analytical Unit, Department of Foreign Affairs and Trade, Australia, 1999, p. 23.

[7] John Minns, "Of Miracles and Models: The Rise and Decline of the Development State in South Korea", *Third World Quarterly*, vol. 22, no. 6, 2001, p. 1034.

[8] Data source: CEIC.

after the outbreak of the crisis. Falling foreign exchange reserves and increasing corporate default led international banks to limit their lending to Korea. Eventually, the government had to accept the International Monetary Fund's policy conditions for the emergency loans needed.

Inadequate Corporate Reform after the Asian Financial Crisis

South Korea's economy suffered from serious recession after the Asian financial crisis. Chaebols' excessive investment overseas made them the main target for blame. Korean chaebols' reforms thus became one of the priorities during the post-crisis period. Chaebols' restructuring after the crisis took the following forms. First was the "five plus three" principles agreed by the government and chaebol leaders to largely enhance chaebols' financial transparency, strengthen shareholders' right and toughen the role of directors. The five principles comprised transparency in accounting and management, resolving mutual debt guarantees among chaebol affiliates, improving firms' financial structure, streamlining business activities and strengthening managers' accountability. The three supplementary principles included regulating chaebols' control of non-bank financial institutions, monitoring circular equity investment by chaebol affiliates, and preventing irregular inheritance arrangements and gift-giving among family members of chaebol owners. Second was the launch of an industrial restructuring programme, known as the Big Deals, to rearrange the core industries of top chaebols and clean up distressed firms. Several chaebols were requested to sell their non-core businesses to other chaebols. [9] Foreign investors were also given preferential privileges to acquire Korean firms. Third was the lifting of many restrictions on mergers and acquisitions (M&A) and FDI to facilitate corporate restructuring. The shares of foreign ownership have increased in the corporate sectors as a result.

---

[9]Mo Jongryn and Moon Chung-in, "Business-Government Relations under Kim Dae-jung", in Stephan Haggard, Lim Wonhyuk and Kim Euysung, *Economic Crisis and Corporate Restructuring in Korea*, Cambridge, Cambridge University Press, 2003, pp. 128-129.

Half of the 30 largest chaebols either went bankrupt or embarked on programmes for corporate reforms by the end of 2000. Numerous chaebol affiliates were sold to foreign investors. Some top chaebol subsidiaries such as Daewoo Motors, Samsung Motors and Sangyong Motors were acquired by multinational companies.[10] The market reforms launched by Kim Dae-jung continued during Roh Moo-hyun administration. Nonetheless, the reforms that aimed at curbing large business's power had limitations due to strong opposition from chaebol leaders. Indeed, the market reforms were not fully implemented. As Kalinowski argued, the post-crisis market reform in South Korea was not to allow the invisible hand to operate the market. Instead, it was rather a political negotiation process between the government, chaebols and other interest groups. In order to compensate chaebols' loss from the post-crisis corporate reforms, the liberalisation of labour market that made laid-off easier was allowed. Meanwhile, foreign investors did not efficiently exercise supervision of corporate governance. Although chaebols followed the principles of shareholder value, they did not surrender family control of their conglomerates to the shareholders.[11]

Despite the concern that post-crisis reform measures might damage Korean conglomerates' profitability, some top chaebols' net profit (gross profit minus operating expenses) has been growing, particularly after the global financial crisis. As shown in Figure 2-2, before 2008, Samsung, Hyundai Motors, LG, SK and Lotte's annual net profits progressed steadily. In 2009, except for Hyundai Motors, the other four chaebols suffered a clear net profit decline. Their net profit however began to surge in 2010. Samsung has had a historically high net profit in 2013 but dipped slightly in 2014 and 2015. Unlike Samsung's expansion, another electronic giant, LG's net profit has fallen since 2011. Hyundai Motor's net profit has also shown considerable expansion since

---

[10] Ha Yong-Chool and Lee Wang Hwi, "The Politics of Economic Reform in South Korea: Crony Capitalism after Ten Years", *Asian Survey*, vol. 47, Issue 6, 2007, pp. 894-914.

[11] T Kalinowski, "The Politics of Market Reforms: Korea's Path from Chaebol Republic to Market Democracy and Back".

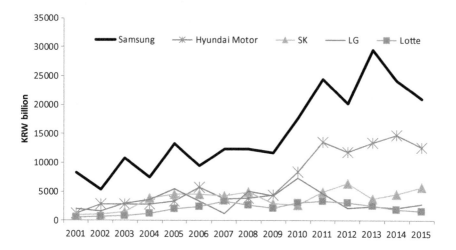

Figure 2-2   South Korea's Top Five Chaebols' Net Profits 2001–2015

Source: Source: Fair Trade Commission, <http://groupopni.ftc.go.kr/> (accessed 17 February 2016).

2011, while SK and Lotte's net profit growth has been decelerating since 2013.

Chaebols have expanded their business power through setting up subsidiaries with different business functions. The number of affiliates owned by the top 30 chaebols was 1,246 in 2012, up from 843 in 2007. The retail giant Lotte Group posted the largest increase in the number of affiliates from 43 at the end of 2007 to 79 in 2012.[12] Although the founding families hold only minority stakes in chaebols' key units, through the complex cross-shareholdings between main companies and their subsidiaries, chaebols continue with their "family style" business operation. The family controlled business practice allows chaebol leaders to benefit financially, giving rise to top earning corporate executives after conglomerates become increasingly

---

[12] "Chaebols Add Many Subsidiaries", *Korea Joongang Daily*, 7 October 2013, <http://koreajoongangdaily.joins.com/news/article/Article.aspx?aid=2978484> (accessed 15 February 2016).

profitable. The 2015 list of richest individuals in South Korea saw a record of 35 US dollar billionaires, up from 21 in 2011 and five in 2009.[13]

To curb chaebol families' power expansion, the ban on new cross-shareholdings between large chaebol affiliates has been instituted since 2014. However, the new rule still allows the present cross-holding structure to remain,[14] implying that the existing family power in certain top chaebols is less likely to be hurt by the new rule.

Chaebols' Expansion in South Korea and Abroad after the Global Financial Crisis

As mentioned, the post-crisis corporate reforms have not been able to constrain chaebols' further expansion. Instead, Korean chaebols' business has stretched further not only in South Korea but also abroad. In particular some top chaebols' business triumphs (such as Samsung and LG) have made the country an important contender in high technology sectors (e.g. mobile phone, flat screen, memory chips, etc) in the world. In 2015, 17 Korean companies were listed in Fortune 500 in terms of total sales revenue (including three in electronics, four in oil, three in automobile, four in services and three in machinery and electric power), progressing from seven in 1990 and 11 in 2005. South Korea now ranks as the seventh country in the world with the largest number of top 500 global companies.[15] Nonetheless, Korean companies' wealth is concentrated in merely a few conglomerates. The "big four", including Samsung, Hyundai Motor, SK Group and LG, accounted for 90% of net profits earned

---

[13] "Korea's 50 Richest People", <http://www.forbes.com/korea-billionaires/#/tab:overall_page:3> (accessed 10 March 2016).

[14] Simon Mundy, "South Korea: Sparks Fly over the Chaebol", *Financial Times*, 2 November 2014, <http://www.ft.com/intl/cms/s/0/9d84d488-5f90-11e4-8c27-00144feabdc0.html> (accessed 22 February 2016).

[15] <http://fortune.com/global500/> (accessed 15 February 2016).

by the top 30 conglomerates in 2013. This is a clear increase of 50%-70% between 2009 and 2012.[16]

As shown in Figure 2-3, top five Korean chaebols' sales revenue (including Samsung, Hyundai Motor, SK, LG and Lotte) accounted for 36%-39% of the country's GDP in 2001 and 2008, and further to 45% in 2009 and 58% in 2015. Chaebols' sales revenue came mostly from exports to overseas countries. In 2015, electrical machinery, vehicles and machinery were South Korea's key export items, accounting for 51% of total exports.[17] Samsung (telecommunication equipment), Hyundai Motor (cars and truck manufacturing), Hynix (semiconductors), Hyundai heavy machinery and LG (consumer electronics) are leading export companies in South Korea.

As exhibited in Table 2-1, Samsung topped the list of the top 20 Korean companies (including chaebols and their affiliates) based on 2013 financial information. In 2013, Samsung's total assets and sales were even greater than the other top four chaebols combined. Samsung had a staff strength of 346,253, which was almost equivalent to the top four combined (359,853). The international business expansion has helped chaebols to enlarge their business empire, especially for the manufacturing giants. In 2013, 86% of Samsung's sales were generated from its overseas markets and only 14% came from its Korean market. The overseas market also dominates in the cases of Hyundai Motor and LG. In comparison, the shares of foreign sales in more service-oriented business groups (e.g. SK and Lotte) are relatively less significant. Following their business expansion in overseas markets, foreign employees took important shares in some chaebols' employment profile. In 2013, the five business groups had 706,106 employees and nearly half of them were hired in foreign countries. The shares of

---

[16] "Top Four Chaebols Generate 90% of South Korean Conglomerate Profits", *Nikkei Asian Review*, 10 April 2014, <http://asia.nikkei.com/magazine/20140410-Growth-Central/Business/Top-four-chaebol-generate-90-of-South-Korean-conglomerate-profits> (accessed 17 February 2016).

[17] Data source: World Trade Atlas.

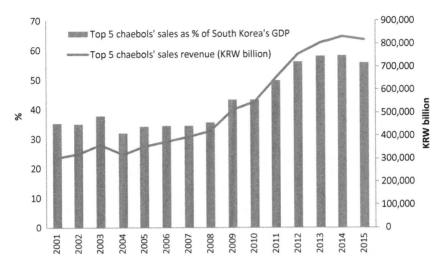

Figure 2-3 Top Five Korean Chaebols' Sales Revenue and Shares in South Korea's GDP 2001–2015

Source: Fair Trade Commission, <http://groupopni.ftc.go.kr/> (accessed 17 February 2016).

Note: The percentages are calculated by the author. Top five chaebols include Samsung, Hyundai Motor, LG, SK and Lotte.

employment in foreign countries were especially high for Samsung and Lotte. Unlike sales and employment, the top five chaebols have most of their assets in South Korea.

Chaebols' significant sales revenue, however, does not translate to contribution to domestic employment. According to official statistics, the top five companies only took 3% of total employment in the country in 2013.[18] Due to the wage dispersion between chaebols and small businesses, chaebols' smaller workforce in Korea has often been blamed for the income inequality. In addition, chaebols' scandals, including accounting fraud, corruption, misbehaviour and chaebol family members' abuse of their position for personal interest, have further damaged their already negative image in Korean society.

---

[18] Data source: *Korea Statistical Yearbook*, 2014.

Table 2-1 Top Five Korean Chaebols' Business Profile in 2013

US$ million and number of persons

	Asset			Sales			Employment		
	As % of total			As % of total			As % of total		
	South Korea	Foreign	Total	South Korea	Foreign	Total	South Korea	Foreign	Total
Samsung	89	11	210,949	14	86	199,500	43	57	346,253
Hyundai Motor	88	12	54,674	39	61	39,495	60	40	104,731
LG	84	16	57,790	19	81	70,281	70	30	96,318
SK	91	9	54,197	52	48	26,762	53	47	93,165
Lotte	88	12	34,262	66	34	27,318	48	52	65,639
Samsung as % of the top 5		51			55			49	

Source: "The Top 20 Korean Multinationals: Changes and Continued Growth of Foreign Investment", Graduate School of International Studies at Seoul National University and the Columbia Centre on Sustainable Investment at the Columbia University, 3 March 2015, < http://ccsi.columbia.edu/files/2015/04/EMGP-Korea-Report-on-2013-FINAL.pdf> (accessed 7 March 2016).

Note: Samsung includes Samsung Electronics Co Ltd, Samsung Display Co Ltd, Samsung C&T Corporation and Samsung SDI Co Ltd; SK includes SK Hynix Inc, SK Telecom Co Ltd, SK Innovation Co Ltd; LG includes LG Chem Ltd, LG Electronics Inc, LG Display Co Ltd; Lotte includes Lotte Chemical Corporation and Lotte Shopping Co. Ltd. The percentages are calculated by the author.

Opinion poll in 2015 showed that 54% of Korean people opposed the pardoning of chaebol leaders.[19] This is unlike a few decades ago when chaebols were considered important in developing the country. As economic benefits are not well distributed, the chaebols-led economic growth cannot win people's support. As such, the government's continuous dependence on chaebols' contributions to sustain the country's economic growth is likely to aggravate social discontent in the country.

Boosting Korean Economy Through "Chaebol-Friendly" Policies

Compared to the 1960s to 1990s, the Korean economy has clearly slowed down since the early 2000s. Subsequent to the global financial crisis, the economy even dwindled to the lowest 0.7% in 2009. The pro-business policies have been considered by the government as imperative to stimulate the Korean economy. These policies however have contributed to the growing strength of chaebols in recent years.

President Lee Myung-bak (2008-2013) vowed to restore the Korean economy by his "Korea7-4-7" plan, reaching 7% of economic growth, US$40,000 of per capita income and making Korea the world's seventh largest economy during his term. To reach these economic goals, several policy measures which benefited chaebol's business expansion were launched. For example, the Lee administration lowered corporate tax rate for large corporations from 25% to 22% in 2008 and further to 20% in 2012. In 2009, the government also abolished the equity investment ceiling system which was considered

---

[19] "Park Grants Pardon to Chaebol Chief", *The Straits Times*, 14 August 2015, <http://www.straitstimes.com/asia/east-asia/park-grants-pardon-to-chaebol-chief> (accessed 23 February 2016); Rose Kim, "For South Korea's Top Students, Chaebols are the Place to Be", *Bloomberg Businessweek*, 26 September 2013, <http://www.bloomberg.com/bw/articles/2013-09-26/for-south-koreas-top-students-chaebol-are-the-place-to-be> (accessed 23 February 2016).

as a hindrance to chaebol's investment expansion.[20] Beyond the favourable policy measures, the government considered amnesty to senior business executives convicted of fraud and assault as necessary for economic revitalisation. From 2008 to 2013, Lee carried out seven rounds of controversial presidential pardons. Several well-known business leaders in large companies, including the chairmen of Hyundai Motor, SK Corp and Hanwha's Group and Samsung Group's president were pardoned.[21] Nonetheless, the pro-chaebol policy measures did not spur Korea's economic growth rates to 7% as expected. South Korea's per capita gross national income reached US$24,696 in 2012,[22] far less than the US$40,000 promised by President Lee. Instead, people's perception is that Lee's policies only increased chaebol's power in the national economy without benefiting the majority of the ordinary people.

Lee's successor, President Park Geun-hye championed "economic democratisation" to reduce the gap between the rich and the poor during the presidential election campaign in 2012. However, when elected, her administration has softened its stance on chaebol's business expansion in order to spur economic growth. In 2015, the Park administration announced reduction of tax audits on large corporations. Tax reduction was also offered for the chaebol practice of funnelling work to affiliates as large companies often argued that strict regulations on funnelling have sapped corporations' desire to invest.[23] Like her predecessor, President Park also pardoned several tycoons of large companies, including SK and Samsung's chairmen, contradicting what she had

---

[20] Even Ramstad, "South Korea Pushes to Curb Conglomerates", *The Wall Street Journal*, 17 October 2012, <http://www.wsj.com/articles/SB100008723963904432 94904578044002698533468> (accessed 17 February 2016).

[21] Simon Mundy, "Lee Criticized over S Korean Pardons", *Financial Times*, 29 January 2013, <http://www.ft.com/intl/cms/s/0/b7f788e4-69c2-11e2-8d07-00144feab49a. html> (accessed 22 February 2016).

[22] Data source: *Korea Statistical Yearbook 2014*, Statistics Korea, February 2015.

[23] "Park Administration Bowing to Chaebol Pressure on Reform Measures", *The Hankyoreh*, 4 August 2013, <http://english.hani.co.kr/arti/english_edition/e_ business/598200.html> (accessed 22 February 2016).

promised during the election campaign. The so-called "one-shot" law, designed to help companies engage in ailing sectors to eliminate excess capacity and improve productivity, has been passed in the parliament and taken effect since August 2016. Firms would be given regulatory relief and tax breaks if their restructuring plans are approved by an evaluation committee. Critics maintain that the law is to help chaebols during the economic difficult times.[24]

Soon after she took office in 2013, President Park announced plans to build a "Creative Economy" which aims to promote a new growth model based on innovation and entrepreneurship. Nonetheless, such an "innovation-driven" economic growth is likely to only enhance the country's reliance on chaebols which accounted for most of the private R&D investments. Chaebol leaders have responded positively to the government's requests to increase domestic investment spending and create employment for domestic workers. Several chaebols have also diversified, expanded or developed new arenas locally. Over the past few years, to become a new pioneer in biopharmaceutical manufacturing in the world, Samsung has made a huge investment of about US$2.7 billion in production plants and research laboratories in biotechnology sectors in South Korea.[25] Hyundai Motor Group has also announced in 2015 that it would spend US$73 billion over four years to expand capacity, build new headquarters and develop new vehicles. About three-quarters of the investment would be made within South Korea.[26] LG also planned to invest more than 10 trillion won (about US$8.7 billion) in building a large plant to produce panels using organic light-emitting diode (OLED) panels. The initial 1.8 trillion

---

[24]"Editorial: One-shot Law", *The Korea Herald*, 10 February 2016, <http://www.koreaherald.com/view.php?ud=20160210000390> (accessed 25 February 2016).

[25]Jonathan Cheng and Lee Min-Jeong, "Samsung's Bet on Biotechnology is Test for Heir Apparent", *The Wall Street Journal*, 17 December 2015, <http://www.wsj.com/articles/samsungs-bet-on-biotechnology-is-test-for-heir-apparent-1450386875> (accessed 26 February 2016).

[26]"Hyundai Motor Group Says to Invest $73 Billion by 2018", Reuters, 6 January 2015, <http://www.reuters.com/article/us-hyundai-motor-investment-idUSKBN0KF0AS20150106> (accessed 26 February 2016).

won (about US$1.6 billion) will be used to build the plant in Paju, South Korea.[27] Heavy investment in R&D is supposed to benefit South Korea's industrial upgrading and maintain its technology superiority ahead of its peers. In fact, given chaebols' rich financial resources, they are more capable of playing an important role in promoting South Korea's transformation towards more innovation- and high technology-driven economy.

In the face of a slowing economy, the Park government tried to rescue the economy and create job opportunities through cooperation with chaebols. However, without clear economic rebound and better wealth distribution, the Park administration's pro-chaebol policy only increased people's doubts about the effectiveness of government-chaebol alliance in the economy. Since 2014, the Park government had been pushing for the "wage peak system" which would cut the wage for senior workers from the age of 56 and encourage companies to hire more young workers with the labour cost saved from reducing the wages of senior workers. By July 2015, nearly half of chaebols and their affiliates had adopted this system. However, the opposition believes that companies will only take advantage of this "wage peak system" to save cost and not to hire more young graduates. The Park administration's labour reform which intends to make the labour market more flexible also encountered strong resistance. The labour reform bills have been stalled since December 2015. The government claimed that reform is to create more jobs for young Koreans and boost the economy while the opposition argued that it will give employers greater leeway in dismissing workers.[28]

---

[27] "South Korea's LG Display to Invest $8.7 in New OLED Plant", Reuters, 26 November 2015, <http://www.reuters.com/article/us-lg-display-investment-idUSK-BN0TF2JY20151127 > (accessed 26 February 2016).

[28] On 14 November 2015, tens of thousands of workers launched street rallies against the labour reform. The protest was also against the government's plan to reintroduce a state-sponsored school textbook. "Korea's Labor Battle", *The Wall Street Journal*,

Plight of Korean SMEs

Unlike chaebols, the numerous SMEs' contribution to economic growth has been less noteworthy. However, it is the SMEs[29] that make the most important contribution to domestic employment. As shown in Table 2-2, in 2012, SMEs accounted for 99.9% of total commercial establishments and hired 87.7% of total labour force in the country. In particular the SMEs in more labour-intensive sectors such as wholesale and retail, accommodation and restaurants, health and social welfare, education services, and repair and individual services employed relatively greater number of workers, or at least 97% of the total labour force in each of the sectors.

Despite SMEs' importance in offering jobs to domestic workers, their limited profit margin constrains their financial resources to upgrade the industry and hire more qualified workers with higher salary. Many young Koreans today would rather stay unemployed than to work in SMEs with inferior wages. That is one of the reasons for the higher unemployment rate for workers aged between 15 and 29 (9.5% in January 2016).[30] Wage dispersion between large companies and SMEs with a bigger workforce has enlarged the income inequality. In 2014, average monthly wage for workers of large companies (more than 300 employees) was 4,645,000 won (US$3,740). In comparison,

---

2 February 2016, <http://www.wsj.com/articles/koreas-labor-battle-1454461279> (accessed 23 February 2016).

[29] South Korean government's definition of SMEs varies by sector. In manufacturing sectors, SME is defined as a company hiring fewer than 300 people with capital of eight billion won or less. In the real estate sectors, SME refers to a company that hires fewer than 50 people with sales worth five billion won or less. Source: Small and Medium Business Administration, South Korea, <http://www.smba.go.kr/eng/smes/statistics_01.do?mc=usr0001148> (accessed 24 February 2016).

[30] "South Korea's Youth Unemployment Hits 16-year High", *Business Standard*, 18 February 2016, <http://www.business-standard.com/article/news-ians/south-korea-s-youth-unemployment-hits-16-year-high-116021800392_1.html> (accessed 24 February 2016).

Table 2-2   SMEs' Shares in Total Number of Firms and Employment in South Korea in 2012

	As % of Total Number of Firms	As % of Total Employees
Agriculture, forestry and fishery	100	100
Mining	99.9	93.5
Manufacturing	99.8	80.4
Electricity, gas, steam and water	97.0	57.2
Sewer/waste treatment, raw material reproduction and environmental restoration	99.5	93.5
Construction	99.8	81.6
Wholesale and retail	99.9	96.6
Transportation	99.9	91.7
Accommodation and restaurants	99.9	98.4
Publishing, video, broadcasting and information service	99.6	79.1
Finance and insurance	98.9	60.1
Real estate and rental	99.7	87.9
Specialised, science and technical service	99.7	75.9
Business facility management and business support service	98.9	65.3
Education service	99.9	96.7
Health and social welfare	99.9	98.7
Art, sport and leisure-related service	99.9	93.0
Repair and other individual service	99.9	97.5
Total industries	**99.9**	**87.7**

Source: Small and Medium Business Administration, <http://www.smba.go.kr/eng/smes/statistics_01.do?mc=usr0001148> (accessed 24 February 2016).

the average monthly wage for workers at SMEs (with 10-29 employees) was 2,698,000 won (US$2,172).[31] The wages of top chaebols were even higher. In 2012, the average monthly wage for workers of Samsung was 4.46 million won (US$3,753), more than double the average monthly

---

[31] Data source: CEIC.

wage for workers with similar skills at SMEs in the electronic industry (two million won or US$1,683).[32] More discussion of income inequality problems will be explored in Chapter 5.

Looking at SMEs' business structure, most SMEs are in wholesale and retail, and accommodation and restaurants which accounted for 48% of the total number of SMEs and 34.5% of total SMEs' employment in 2012 (Table 2-3). In comparison SMEs in higher value-added service sectors have relatively fewer shares in total employment (such as in finance and insurance, publishing, video, broadcasting and information service, specialised, science and technical service, business facility management and business support service, etc).

Due to SMEs' high concentration in wholesale and retail, accommodation and restaurant, the trend for second- and third-generation chaebol families to open bakeries and other small food outlets in recent years raised concerns about the threat it poses to the livelihoods of small store owners. With the support of their parents' business empires, these shops were placed in hotels, department stores and other large buildings with good locations and sales. When the retail business ran by chaebols' young family members was flourishing, the number of bakeries ran by self-employed individuals plunged significantly from about 18,000 in 2003 to around 4,000 in 2011 according to the Korea Federation of Small and Medium Business.[33]

Even with the massive relocation of production overseas since the 1990s, many SMEs still retain their manufacturing business in South Korea. In 2012, 10.7% in SMEs were in the manufacturing sectors

---

[32] The average monthly wages for workers excluded wages for managers in both Samsung and SMEs. Han Jiwon, Liem Wol-san and Lee Yoomi, "In the Belly of the Beast: Samsung Electronics' Supply Chain and Work Force in South Korea", Asia Monitor Resource Centre, 2013, <http://old.amrc.org.hk/system/files/3%20 Samsung%20Electronics%E2%80%99%20Supply%20Chain%20and%20 Workforce%20in%20South%20Korea.pdf> (accessed 6 March 2016).

[33] Kim So-Hyun, "Korea's Chaebol Scion Slammed for Running Coffee Shops, Import Business", *The Korea Herald*, 28 January 2012, <http://news.asiaone.com/ News/AsiaOne%2BNews/Asia/Story/A1Story20120128-324406.html> (accessed 23 February 2016).

Table 2-3   Breakdown of South Korea's SMEs by Sector in 2012

	As % of Total No. of Firms at SMEs	As % of Total Employees at SMEs
Agriculture, forestry and fishery	0.0002	0.1
Mining	0.1	0.1
Manufacturing	**10.7**	**22.7**
Electricity, gas, steam and water	0.0001	0.1
Sewer/waste treatment, raw material reproduction and environmental restoration	0.2	0.4
Construction	3.2	6.5
Wholesale and retail	**27.9**	**20.2**
Transportation	**10.8**	**6.7**
Accommodation and restaurants	**20.1**	**14.3**
Publishing, video, broadcasting and information service	0.9	2.4
Finance and insurance	0.3	0.8
Real estate and rental	3.3	2.0
Specialised, science and technical service	2.3	3.9
Business facility management and business support service	1.2	4.1
Education service	4.4	3.7
Health and social welfare	2.9	5.0
Art, sport and leisure-related service	2.9	1.9
Repair and other individual service	8.9	4.9
Total industries	**100**	**100**

Source: Small and Medium Business Administration, <http://www.smba.go.kr/eng/smes/statistics_01.do?mc=usr0001148> (accessed 24 February 2016).

which contributed 22.7% to total employment in SMEs (Table 2-3). Nonetheless, the weak Japanese yen and soft external demand have badly hurt the SMEs in manufacturing in recent years. Korea International Trade Association's survey showed that 95% of SMEs' business was negatively impacted by the weak yen. Exports by SMEs fell 3.9% between

2009 and 2013.[34] The business disintegration between domestic SMEs and chaebols in manufacturing production also explains why the SMEs did not benefit from chaebols' business expansion. In 2011, estimates have it that the top 15 chaebols purchased 44% of raw materials and parts from their own subsidiaries.[35]

The Korean government has been aware of the importance of SMEs in providing job opportunities for domestic workers and in equalising economic benefits since the 1980s. However, policy initiatives for supporting Korean SMEs since more than two decades ago did not effectively boost their development. In recent years, several policies have been adopted to encourage SMEs' innovation, promote their export growth and help them adapt to the globalisation trend. When Park took office, she also launched several programmes to provide financial assistance to SMEs and start-up firms. Although supporting measures for SMEs continue to remain in place, to maintain Korea's economic growth, the Lee and Park administrations did not withdraw their pro-chaebol policies. Hence, SMEs continue to struggle when expanding their business in an economy largely dominated by chaebols.

Conclusion

Chaebols' importance in driving South Korea's exports-led economic growth can be traced back to the 1960s when Park Chung-Hee's government heavily financed chaebols to boost the country's exports. Hence, chaebols' business success has since paved the way for the country to become an important world manufacturer in heavy industries such as shipbuilding, automobile and steel production. By setting up entry

---

[34] Kang Tae-jun, "South Korea's SMEs Struggle to Compete", *Financial Times*, 25 November 2014, <http://blogs.ft.com/beyond-brics/2014/11/25/south-koreas-smes-struggle-to-compete/ > (accessed 24 February 2016).

[35] Kwak Jung-soo, "Chaebol Getting More Power as They Contribute Less to the Economy", *The Hankyoreh*, 9 July 2014, <http://english.hani.co.kr/arti/english_edition/e_business/646183.html> (accessed 29 February 2016).

barriers to selected manufacturing industries and giving financial privileges to certain large firms, the chaebol-led "miracle on the Han River" had been shaped during Park Chung-Hee's administration in the 1960s and 1970s. Nonetheless, chaebols' development after the 1980s has become uncontrollable by the government. The greater business expansion in international market further strengthened their financial muscles and dominance in Korea's economy. Although severely hit by the Asian financial crisis, those that survive grew even larger than before the crisis. Even with the post-crisis corporate reforms, through cross-shareholdings between main companies and their subsidiaries, the founding families continue to be chaebols' main stakeholders. The wage dispersion between large and small firms has raised concerns about the growing income inequality. Nonetheless, short-term economic growth goal prevails. To stimulate the Korean economy, both Lee Myung-bak and Park Geun-hye governments launched several pro-large business policies that benefited chaebols' business operation.

Although chaebols are more capable than SMEs in realising South Korea's innovation-driven economic growth, the chaebol-dominated high technology development may not benefit everyone in the country. The less qualified workers will suffer if the high valued-added sectors dominate the economy. Increasing productivity also implies that fewer workers will be needed. As a consequence, more people will be unemployed.

More importantly, Korean chaebols' long-term sustainability could be challenged by their non-transparent corporate governance and less matured global business management. Unlike other MNCs which emphasise mostly shareholders' right, internal commercial dealings between chaebols and their affiliates continue to take place. Relying on only a handful of large companies with relatively poor corporate governance for its economic survival will certainly put South Korea's economic future at high risk. The government will have to implement initiatives to foster small businesses. However, both Lee Myung-bak and Park Geun-hye administrations could not afford to abandon economic policies that are short-term and chaebol-oriented. Encouraging FDI may help to balance the polarised domestic economic structure.

Huge FDI in both manufacturing and services will make up for the limited job supply from chaebols. Korean SMEs can also benefit from FDI from advanced countries to upgrade their technology, product quality and management skills. The government will have to construct a more market-oriented business environment for both domestic and foreign firms to compete. More financial assistance and welfare expenditure are needed as the less competitive sectors and less qualified workers will suffer greatly from the country's greater economic opening up in the future.

Chapter 3

South Korea-United States
Free Trade Agreement

The implementation of the KORUS since 2012 has been a significant event in South Korea's history of foreign trade policy. Not only does it pave the way for greater access of South Korean firms to the most important consumption market in the world, it also further strengthens the country's security alliance with the United States. For the United States, the bilateral FTA is the second largest FTA that it has signed, after NAFTA (North American Free Trade Agreement) in terms of total goods traded. The FTA opens up new opportunities for the United States to expand its market share in South Korea, in particular, agricultural products and services. It also serves as a model for other Asian countries to set up similar institutionalised economic relations with the United States in the future. KORUS FTA would thus help deepen US engagement in Asia-Pacific economic regionalism. The only setback is the increased competition between Korean and American firms. Without appropriate remedial measures and adjustments, the less competitive workers and sectors in both countries would likely suffer from the effects of the FTA.

This chapter offers an analytical review of the ratification process, the main content of KORUS FTA and the impact on bilateral economic relations. It will cover five major areas: the motivation for proceeding with a bilateral FTA; South Korean and American economic features and the mutual economic gains after implementation;

major FTA rules; bilateral trade and investment relations after the KORUS; and the implications of the KORUS FTA on East Asian economic regionalism. The conclusion will sum up the main points and arguments raised in this chapter.

The Need for the KORUS FTA

The KORUS FTA was brought to the table as early as in the mid-1980s. The discussions met with some hiccups over sensitive issues on agriculture and service industries and were held back.[1] It was not until 2004 that the two sides reached a consensus on initiating bilateral FTA negotiations. After years of meetings and exchanges, the two countries proceeded with official negotiations in 2006 and 2007.[2] On 30 June 2007, the KORUS FTA was officially signed in Seoul.

The KORUS FTA was a pillar of then President Roh Moo-hyun's (2003–2008) economic reform plan. Before the KORUS FTA, Korea has signed FTAs with only a few smaller economies, such as Singapore, Chile, EFTA and ASEAN. The economic effect might have been limited due to these economies' relatively insignificant share in Korea's trade and investment. The FTAs with larger economies and with high quality trade measures were considered more vital for the country's economic advancement. In 2003, the Roh administration released "FTA Promotion Road Map" to set FTAs with large economies his priorities. As an export-led economy, South Korea hopes to secure greater access to the US market, the biggest consumer in the world. Although Korean export values to the United States had gradually increased over the last few decades, its shares in US total imports registered a slight decline from 3.3% in 2000 to 2.3% in 2008.[3] South Korean manufacturers' dependence on overseas production might

---

[1] Inkyo Cheong, "Economic Assessment of the Korea-US FTA", *Korean Social Sciences Review*, vol. 2, no. 1, 2012, pp. 33–94.

[2] Inkyo Cheong, "Economic Assessment of the Korea-US FTA".

[3] Data source: US Bureau of Economic Analysis.

have reduced Korea's direct export to America. The growing competition as a result of an overlap with its regional peers' exports was another downward push. South Korea is competing with Japan in automobiles and with Taiwan, Thailand, China and other Asian countries in ICT products. In particular China's quick industrial catch up poses a serious threat to Korea's export prospect.

To improve South Korea service sectors' competitiveness is another motivation for signing the FTA. After Korean firms' relocation of manufacturing factories overseas, services gradually took a large share in the Korean economy. However, services are less competitive than manufacturing sectors and are less able to sustain the country's economic growth after the manufacturing's hollowing out. The Roh government firmly believed that the competitiveness of service sectors can be largely improved by realising FTAs with advanced countries. KORUS FTA was regarded as an important measure to facilitate FDI from the United States. Korean companies in services would benefit from the competition and be propelled to improve on their competitiveness. After he stepped down in 2007, Roh's successor President Lee Myung-bak (2008–2013) continued to support KORUS as a part of his plan to promote the country's economic growth.

For the United States, South Korea's 50 million population is an important market for its agricultural and pharmaceutical products, Intellectual Property Right (IPR) and financial services. However, South Korea's low level of openness for products in which the United States holds competitive advantages was a concern.

Politically, the KORUS FTA is also a bridge to strengthen the bilateral security alliance in the face of political uncertainties in the Korean Peninsula. For the United States, the nexus between FTAs and its geopolitical interests has been tightly connected especially after the 911 attack in 2001. An FTA with South Korea would give Washington a strong position to maintain its strategic and economic presence in the region increasingly dominated by China. The implementation of the KORUS FTA was expected to further hasten Japan to enter into trade negotiations with the United States, which had been stalled due to opposition from its domestic agricultural groups.[4] The FTA with South Korea was considered a facilitator of US involvement in East Asia's rapid development of economic regionalism and could reinforce its role as a stabiliser in the region.

Despite these advantages, the ratification process in the two countries took longer than expected. After signing the FTA in 2007, it took almost five years for the agreement to be put into force eventually. The opposition parties in South Korea and the United States considered the FTA as not in their country's interests and objected to its ratification in the parliament. The two most contentious issues involved the agriculture and automobile industries. Even when the public protested against unsafe US beef quarantine standard, the Lee Ming-bak administration went ahead to open the Korean market to US beef before his visit to the United States in April 2008. Speculations were rife that President Lee sacrificed public health in exchange for his visit to America.[5] In the meantime, the opposition in the United States believed that the KORUS FTA did not go far enough to break down South Korea's trade barriers and could not address US auto trade imbalance problems with South Korea. US automakers' demand for more concession was rejected by the Korean side.

In spite of the many controversies, the two countries' close connection in the political, economic, military and diplomatic fields made ratification only a matter of time. Politicians were aware that the failure to ratify the bilateral FTA could impact not only the economic sectors but also overall relations. Security concerns eventually pushed the two countries to renegotiate on the trade deal. After the Cheonan incident (South Korea navy sinking) in March 2010 and North Korea's sudden artillery attacks on South Korea in November of the same year, the urgent need to cement security alliance to tackle the growing threat from the North propelled the two countries to relaunch stalled trade

---

[4]Sohn Yul and Koo Min Gyo, "Securitizing Trade: The Case of the Korea-US Free Trade Agreement", *International Relations of the Asia-Pacific*, vol. 11, 2011, pp. 433–460.
[5]Yul Sohn and Koo Min Gyo, "Securitizing Trade".

negotiations.[6] On 3 December 2010, US President Obama and South Korea President Lee Myung-bak announced consensus on the outstanding issues in the FTA. The final agreement saw Korea granting further concessions on automobile and agricultural issues. The agreement was passed by the US congress on 12 October 2011 and by the Korea National Assembly on 22 November of the same year.

South Korea and the US Economy in Complementarity

Prior to the KORUS FTA's entry into force, several studies estimated the potential positive effect of the agreement on both the US and Korean economies. Using different economic models, the forecast for future economic growth and welfare gain for the two countries varies. Given South Korea's small economic size, more protected market and foreign trade reliance, it was estimated that South Korea's overall economy is the bigger beneficiary of this FTA even though several small Korean businesses in less competitive sectors would suffer greatly from the economic opening up.[7] US agricultural products were expected to have much to gain from the trade deal as South Korea's tariffs on agricultural imports before the FTA were high.

The economic complementarity between the two countries explains the benefits they gain in different sectors after the free trade deal. In general, the United States is a bigger market for consumption goods than the Korean market. The latter has relied on exporting manufacturing goods in exchange for more advanced technology and services imported from the United States. The different comparative advantage can be seen from their dissimilar economic structure. As shown in Table 3-1, in

---

[6]"S. Korea's Final Report Affirms Cheonan Was Sunk by N. Korean Torpedo", *CNN News*, 14 September 2010, <http://edition.cnn.com/2010/WORLD/asiapcf/09/13/south.korea.cheonan.report/> (accessed 30 August 2016).
[7]Bill Cooper and Mark Manyin, "The Proposed South Korea-US Free Trade Agreement (KORUS FTA): Problems and Prospects", *International Journal of Korean Studies*, vol. X, no. 1, 2006, pp. 101–140.

Table 3-1   Major Economic Indicators of South Korea and the United States in 2015

	South Korea	United States
1. Domestic production		
GDP growth rate (%)	2.6	2.4
GDP (US$ billion)	1,377	17,947
GDP per capita (US$)	27,195	55,805
As % of GDP Agriculture	2.8	2.8
Manufacturing	31.0	18.9
Services	66.2	78.3
2. Labour force		
As % of total Agriculture	4.0	1.3
employment Manufacturing	18.0	12.0
Services	78.0	81.0
Nonagricultural self-employed	n/a	5.7
Unemployment rate (%)	3.6	5.3
Employment (million persons)	25.9	148.8
3. External trade		
Total trade balance in goods (US$ billion)	90	−746
Main merchandise export items (as % of total exports)	Electrical machinery (26%)	Machinery (13%)
	Vehicles, not railway (13%)	Electrical machinery (11%)
	Machinery (12%)	Aircraft, spacecraft (9%)
Main merchandise import items (as % of total imports)	Mineral fuel, oil, etc (24%)	Electrical machinery (15%)
	Electrical machinery (18%)	Machinery (14%)
	Optical medical instruments (11%)	Vehicles, not railway (13%)
Total trade balance in services (US$ billion)	−15.7	262
Main service export items (as % of total service exports)	Transport (33%)	Travel (27%)
	Other business services (20%)	Other business services (18%)
	Travel (15%)	IPR (17%)
Main service import items (as % of total service imports)	Other business services (26%)	Travel (23%)
	Transport (26%)	Other business services (20%)
	Travel (21%)	Transport (20%)

Source: International Monetary Fund, World Economic Outlook Database, April 2016; CEIC; World Trade Atlas; US Bureau of Labour Statistics; and Korean Statistical Information Services.

2015, the United States' GDP amounted to US$17,947 billion, which was 13 times larger than Korea's. Services contributed 78.3% of total GDP in the United States while manufacturing and agriculture accounted for 18.9% and 2.8% respectively. Although services also took a large share in South Korea's GDP (66.2%), the manufacturing production stood at a relatively strong 31% compared to the manufacturing share in the United States' GDP.

The labour force structure of the two countries shows greater employment shares in services than in manufacturing. In South Korea, the lower percentage of employment in manufacturing (18%) compared to manufacturing's share in GDP (31%) is a product of its high dependence on overseas production. The mass employment at home shifted to services with lower wages after manufacturing sectors' hollowing out. As a result, the services' share in South Korea's GDP is not as high as that in the United States even though the percentages in service employment in both countries are quite close (78% in South Korea and 81% in the United States).

South Korea's comparative advantage is in its external trade; the greater export of merchandise goods than imports explains its trade surplus in goods. South Korea and the United States share a few similar merchandise export items, such as machinery and electrical machinery. While South Korea exports mostly vehicles, the United States exports more aircraft and spacecraft, a reflection of the different level of technological sophistication in manufactured goods for exports. Being a resource poor country, South Korea is dependent on importing mineral fuel for its domestic use. It also imports a great share of high technology intensity products (eg. optical and medical instruments) from advanced countries. In comparison, the United States is less dependent on foreign mineral fuel and oil imports than South Korea. It imports mostly manufactured items that are high labour-intensive or middle technology-intensive products. Foreign vehicles also take a large portion of the US market.

Unlike South Korea, the United States specialises in providing services and enjoys a substantial trade surplus with the world. In services exports, "transport", "other business services" and "travel" are the important export and import items for South Korea. Transport services cover the process of carriage of people and objects from one location to another, and related supporting and auxiliary services whereas travel encompasses a range of goods and services consumed by non-residents in the economy that they visit. Other business services are merchanting trade and other trade-related services.[8] South Korea's service exports items are also important service trade items for the United States. The only difference is that the United States has considerable export of IPR to other countries which makes up its third largest export items after "other business services" and "travel". Product, industrial processes and designs with patents, trademarks, copyrights, trade secrets and franchises would be charged for IPR to the licencees. US comparative advantage in IPR explains its emphasis and inclusion in KORUS FTA as well as trade deals with other countries.

Key Provisions in KORUS FTA

The KORUS FTA proposes to achieve massive trade liberalisation by removing 90% of tariffs for manufactured products in three years and eventually all of them in the future. South Korea's major export items such as automobiles, electronics and semiconductors are not expected to benefit much since US tariffs on these goods are already low, ranging from 0% to 2.5%.[9] For the United States, upon the implementation of KORUS, almost 80% of US exports to Korea of consumer and industrial products became duty free on 15 March 2012, and nearly 95% of bilateral trade in consumer and industrial products will become duty free within five years. For agricultural products, the Agreement has immediately eliminated tariffs and quotas on a broad range of

---

[8]According to the United Nations' definition, "merchanting trade" is the purchase of goods by a resident of the compiling economy from a non-resident and the subsequent resale of the goods to another non-resident. During the process, the goods do not enter or leave the compiling economy. *Manual on Statistics of International Trade in Services*, United Nations, 2002, p. 47.

[9]Lee Yong-Shik, Lee Jaemin and Sohn Kyung Han, "The United States-Korea Free Trade Agreement: Path to Common Economic Prosperity or False Promise", *East Asia Law Review*, vol. 6, issue 1, pp. 111–162, <http://scholarship.law.upenn.edu/cgi/viewcontent.cgi?article=1051&context=ealr> (accessed 22 June 2016).

products, with nearly two-thirds (by value) of Korea's agricultural imports from the United States becoming duty free. Tariffs and import quotas on most other agricultural products would be phased out in 10 years.[10] South Korea also agreed to eliminate its 40% tariff on beef muscles imported from the United States over a 15-year period.[11]

The KORUS FTA composed of 24 chapters and three annexes. Except for the basic FTA measures, such as "national treatment", "rule of origin", "customs administration and trade facilitation", "sanitary and phytosanitary measures" and "trade remedies", the KORUS FTA encompassed a variety of "high standard" measures. As shown in Table 3-2, the KORUS FTA is a comprehensive and high quality agreement with state-of-the-art regulations on e-commerce, telecommunications, financial services, labour, environment, competition and IPR. A high quality KORUS could serve as a springboard for South Korea to reach the level of an advanced economy that adheres to global rules and standards.[12] On the other hand, the wide range of FTA provisions is expected to bring South Korea in line with US rules and hence create a favourable business environment for Americans doing business in South Korea. For South Korea, this would necessitate changes to a variety of domestic rules and practices, including the enforcement of IPR, protection of foreign investors, establishment of environmental and labour standard, transparency in the application of domestic laws and regulations, and the establishment of an investment dispute settlement mechanism outside the national court systems.[13] Protectionism is minimised in the affected sectors as the Korean government has to be

---

[10] Brock R Williams, Mark E Manyin, Remy Jurenas and Michaela D Platzer, "The US-South Korea Free Trade Agreement (KORUS FTA): Provisions and Implementation", *CRS Report*, 16 September 2014, pp. 1–50, <https://www.fas.org/sgp/crs/row/RL34330.pdf> (accessed 30 May 2016).

[11] Brock R. Williams, Mark E. Manyin, Remy Jurenas and Michaela D. Platzer, "The US-South Korea Free Trade Agreement (KORUS FTA)", pp. 1–50.

[12] Inkyo Cheong, "Evaluation of the Korea-US FTA and Implications for East Asian Economic Integration", *The Journal of East Asia Affairs*, vol. 21, no. 2, pp. 1–26.

[13] Lee Yong-Shik, Lee Jaemin and Sohn Kyung Han, "The United States-Korea Free Trade Agreement", <http://scholarship.law.upenn.edu/cgi/viewcontent.cgi?article=1051&context=ealr> (accessed 22 June 2016).

Table 3-2   Summary of the KORUS FTA

Preamble	The two sides recognise their longstanding and strong partnership and desire to strengthen close economic relations
Chapter 1	Initial Provisions and Definitions
Chapter 2	National Treatment and Market Access for Goods
Chapter 3	Agriculture
Chapter 4	Textiles and Apparels
Chapter 5	Pharmaceuticals and Medical Devices
Chapter 6	Rules of Origin and Origin Procedures
Chapter 7	Customs Administration and Trade Facilitation
Chapter 8	Sanitary and Phytosanitary Measures
Chapter 9	Technical Barriers to Trade
Chapter 10	Trade Remedies
Chapter 11	Investment
Chapter 12	Cross-Border Trade in Services
Chapter 13	Financial Services
Chapter 14	Telecommunications
Chapter 15	Electronic Commerce
Chapter 16	Competition-Related Matters
Chapter 17	Government Procurement
Chapter 18	Intellectual Property Rights
Chapter 19	Labour
Chapter 20	Environment
Chapter 21	Transparency
Chapter 22	Institutional Provisions and Dispute Settlement
Chapter 23	Exceptions
Chapter 24	Final Provisions
Annex	Annex I: Non-Conforming Measures for Services and Investment Annex II: Non-Conforming Measures for Services and Investment Annex III: Non-Conforming Measures for Financial Services General Notes, Tariff Schedules and TRQ Annexes

Source: Office of the United States Trade Representative, <https://ustr.gov/trade-agreements/free-trade-agreements/korus-fta/final-text> (accessed 23 June 2016).

fair to both foreign and domestic companies and has to adopt a free business competition environment for both Korean and American entrepreneurs.

For the agricultural sector, one of the most controversial issues during the bilateral trade negotiations, the United States had demanded for the removal of all tariffs and non-tariff barriers to its agricultural products. These requests were difficult for South Korea to accept. Korea's agricultural sector in most product groups is less competitive than that of the United States. Opening up Korea's agricultural market would put Korean farmers' livelihood at risk though consumers would benefit from the cheaper agricultural imports. The public was particularly concerned about the "mad cow disease" detected in US beef which has been banned since December 2003. Lee Myung-bak government's decision to reopen the market for US beef was boycotted by the public. The Lee government attempted to calm public anger by positioning the KORUS FTA as in the interests of Korea's future economic prosperity. In the final stage of negotiation, Korea agreed to open up its market for US agricultural products except rice.

Textiles were another key issue in the FTA negotiation. Since Korea is a net exporter of textile products to the United States, it requested the United States to increase access and relax its rule of origin. The United States demanded the adoption of a special safeguard in order to minimise the impact on its domestic textile manufacturers from the potential quick increase of textile imports from South Korea after the implementation of the bilateral FTA. Eventually both agreed to eliminate all Korean tariffs on 77% (by value) of US exports of textiles and apparel. In response, the United States has immediately eliminated tariffs on 52% (by value) of Korean textile and apparel imports.[14]

A number of regulatory issues were raised on the service sector during the negotiations to facilitate US firms' entry to the Korean market. According to the KORUS FTA, services in financial, telecommunication, international delivery, legal consultancy and electronic commerce

---

[14] "Industry by the Numbers", US Korea Connect, <http://www.uskoreaconnect.org/business-connect/industry-numbers/textiles.html> (accessed 30 August 2016).

are opened to US investments and compete with local Korean companies. The agreement also contains government procurement provisions in which the two countries agree to open their procurement markets to the other party. Before the FTA, accessibility to the other party's procurement market had been limited by its exclusiveness to foreign suppliers. Chapter 17 of the KORUS FTA thus attempts to expand its criteria to require the two countries to open more government contracts to the other party. The opening up measure includes more items than what has been listed in the government procurement agreement under the WTO.[15]

The IPR provision is another important advancement in the bilateral economic opening-up measures that exceeds the Agreement on Trade-Related Aspects of Intellectual Property Rights (TRIPS) under the WTO. For example, the duration of copyright is now 70 years after the death of the writer, more than the 50 years under TRIPS. The trademark protection under the FTA extends to not only certification of conventional marks for trade but also sound and scent.[16]

South Korea-US Trade Development after KORUS FTA

Bilateral trade has steadily increased after the KORUS FTA took effect in 2012. In 2015, two-way goods trade between South Korea and the United States totalled US$114 billion, a rise from US$101 billion in 2011. This made the United States South Korea's second largest export destination and third largest import origin. South Korea is America's seventh largest export destination and sixth largest import origin.

---

[15] Chung Hong-Sik, "Government Procurement in the United States-Korea Free Trade Agreement: Great Opportunities for Both Sides?" *Northwestern Journal of International Law and Business*, vol. 34, issue 2, 2014, pp. 299–335, <http://scholarlycommons.law.northwestern.edu/cgi/viewcontent.cgi?article=1760&context=njilb> (accessed 1 July 2016).

[16] Lee Yong-Shik, Lee Jaemin and Sohn Kyung Han, "The United States-Korea Free Trade Agreement".

Service trade volume has developed relatively insignificantly compared to trade in goods. In 2015, bilateral service trade amounted to US$34 billion, a slow expansion from US$26 billion in 2011.[17]

South Korea's trade balance with the United States shows that the FTA seems to have reinforced bilateral trade based on the two countries' respective comparative advantages: South Korea in manufacturing and the United States in services. The FTA thus allows South Korea to export more manufactured goods to the United States, while granting American service providers greater access to Korean market. Beyond the tariff cut and greater investment liberalisation under the KORUS FTA, the moderate growth of US economy after the global financial crisis is another factor for the stronger trade relations between the two countries after the implementation of KORUS FTA. In 2015, the United States registered a solid 2.5% economic growth, from −2.8% in 2009. Its unemployment rate also declined from nearly 10% in 2010 to 5.2% in 2015 according to the data from the International Monetary Fund. The decent economic growth allowed the United States to import more goods from South Korea. As shown in Figure 3-1, South Korea's merchandise trade surplus with the United States doubled from US$11.6 billion in 2011 to US$25.8 billion in 2015. However, the sluggish economy in South Korea in recent years may have restrained the Korean consumption of US goods. The limited wage increase has also restrained Korean consumers' purchasing capacity.

US official document indicated that certain US export items, such as passenger vehicles, pharmaceuticals and machinery have evident growth after the FTA. In particular, US auto exports to South Korea increased by 208% between 2011 and 2015, more rapid than US auto exports to the world by more than 14 times.[18] Some agricultural products to South Korea (such as beef, lemons, shelled almonds fresh

---

[17] Data source: US Bureau of Economic Analysis.

[18] "Fact Sheet: Four Year Snapshot: The US-Korea Free Trade Agreement", Office of the United States Trade Representative, 2016, <https://ustr.gov/about-us/policy-offices/press-office/fact-sheets/2016/March/Four-Year-Snapshot-KORUS> (accessed 30 June 2016).

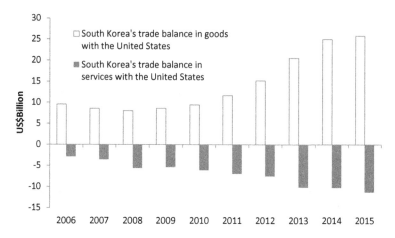

Figure 3-1   South Korea's Trade Balance with the United States 2006–2015

Source: CEIC and US Bureau of Economic Analysis.

cheese, cherries and alcohols) also have clear export growth according to the statistics from United States Trade Representative. Indeed, South Korea has been an important agricultural exports market for America. In 2015, South Korea ran US$5.2 billion of trade deficit in food and animal products with the United States. Despite US export growth for certain products, overall bilateral trade was in South Korea's favour. Major sources of Korean trade surplus items such as vehicles, machinery mineral fuel and oil have had clear growth during 2013 and 2015 while electrical machinery had had slight decline from 2014 to 2015 (Table 3-3). Even with the increasing sales of US passenger cars in South Korea, the bilateral trade imbalance in automobiles continued to develop, indicating that South Korea has sold more cars to the United States than vice versa. In 2006, automobiles accounted for 75% of total Korean trade surplus with the United States. In 2015, the ratio increased to 86%.[19] Meanwhile, South Korea's trade deficit in optical and medical instruments, aircraft and spacecraft with the United States has visible growth. Overall, South Korea's trade surplus

---

[19] Data source: World Trade Atlas.

Table 3-3   South Korea's Trade Balance with the United States by Major Trade Items

US$ million

Trade in goods	2013	2014	2015
1. Vehicles, Not Railway (HS Code 87)	17,002	19,718	22,247
2. Electrical Machinery (HS Code 85)	6,059	6,254	5,709
3. Machinery (HS Code 84)	3,853	3,865	4,431
4. Mineral Fuel, Oil, etc (HS Code 27)	1,782	500	1,200
5. Optical and medical instruments (HS Code 90)	−2,003	−1,962	−2,302
6. Aircraft and Spacecraft (HS Code 88)	−1,236	−465	−1,531
Trade in services	**2012**	**2013**	**2014**
1. Maintenance and repair services	n/a	−580	−646
2. Transport	2,732	3,148	3,349
3. Travel (for all purposes including education)	−4,642	−5,345	−6,548
4. Insurance services	−201	−188	−194
5. Financial services	−721	−729	−656
6. Charges for the use of intellectual property	−5,383	−7,144	−5,929
7. Telecommunications, computer, and information services	−206	−253	−267
8. Other business services	n/a	−1,299	−1,566
9. Government goods and services	2,285	2,229	2,226

Source: World Trade Atlas and US Bureau of Economic Analysis.

items have grown more noticeable than its trade deficit items with America.

Unlike bilateral merchandise trade, South Korea service trade deficit with the United States enlarged from US$6.9 billion to US$11.3 billion from 2006 to 2015. This reflects US comparative advantage in services and the bilateral FTA has strengthened this comparative advantage vis-à-vis South Korea. South Korea only ran trade surplus in transport services and government goods and services with the United States while other service trade items were in deficit (Table 3-3). From 2012 to 2014, South Korea's trade surplus in transport service experienced clear growth whereas government goods and services saw a slight decline. Travel service is South Korea's largest source of service trade deficit with the United States at US$6.5 billion in 2014, followed by "charges for the use of intellectual property" at US$5.9 billion. The trade deficit in travel service reflects greater Korean tourist expenditures in the United States than vice versa after the KORUS FTA has taken effect. The growing deficit in "charges for the use of intellectual property" shows US technology superiority over that of South Korea.

Bilateral Investment Relations after the KORUS FTA

US investment in South Korea began to show progress after Korea has undertaken reforms on account of the Asian financial crisis to promote inward FDI. However, the United States still considered the overall business environment in South Korea as not friendly for foreign investors. Prior to the KORUS FTA, South Korea's restriction on foreign investment in key sectors and lack of protection for IPR had often been criticised by the United States. Under the KORUS FTA, these restrictions have been relaxed with the inclusion of the non-discriminatory national treatment, most-favoured nation (MFN) treatment and minimum standard of treatment in the FTA. Overall, the KORUS FTA has increased investment opportunities for American and Korean companies by providing them with a conducive regulatory environment and stronger investor protection.

The effect of KORUS FTA on mutual investment is noticeable. As exhibited in Figure 3-2, US investment in South Korea increased steadily from a low of US$22.4 billion in 2008 to US$34.9 billion in 2014. American investors in South Korea centred their investments in the manufacturing sectors, followed by the financial sector. Conversely, in 2006, Korea's investment in America was only a third of US investment in South Korea. South Korea's investment in America had grown from US$9.5 billion in 2006 to US$19.9 billion in 2011. In 2014, South Korean investment in the United States (US$36 billion) outstripped US investment in South Korea (US$34.9 billion), mostly in wholesale trade. Although overall investment from the United States is relatively less significant than Korean investment in the United States, America

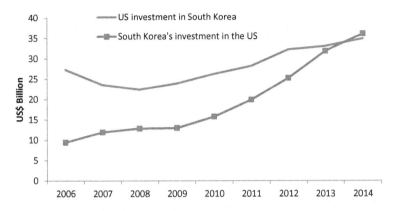

Figure 3-2   Bilateral Investment between South Korea and the United States 2006–2014

Source: US Bureau of Economic Analysis.

has remained the leading foreign investor in South Korea. During 2012–2014, US investment accounted for nearly 20% of total FDI in Korea, a slight increase from 19% during 2009–2011.[20]

America's huge consumption market has contributed to Korean investors' interest in wholesale trade sectors in the United States. Korean manufacturing's investment in the United States has also seen clear improvement after the FTA took effect (Table 3-4). The productive and highly educated workers are a US advantage for attracting Korean investment in professional, scientific and technical services, and manufacturing sectors. The low interest rate in the United States is a motivating factor for Korea's investment in real estate as part of its investment diversification strategy.[21] Indeed, the investment in the United States is not for Korean companies' profits alone. According to US official statistics in 2016, Korean-owned firms in the United States

---

[20] Data source: Korea Exim Bank.

[21] "Korean Financial Companies Increasing Investment in American Commercial Real Estate Market", *Business Korea*, 8 September 2016, <http://www.businesskorea.co.kr/english/news/money/15797-opposite-direction-korean-financial-companies-increasing-investment-american> (accessed 12 September 2016).

Table 3-4   Accumulated Bilateral Investment by Sector 2009–2014

	US Investment in South Korea (US$ billion)			South Korea Investment in the US (US$ billion)		
	2009–2011	2012–2014	Change (%)	2009–2011	2012–2014	Change (%)
Manufacturing	37.8	27.7	−26.8	6.4	12.3	108.1
Wholesale trade	4.7	4.3	−7	38.1	67.8	78.0
Information	0.9	1	8.8	0.02	n/a	n/a
Finance	19.7	15.2	−22.9	0.2	0.3	90.2
Professional, scientific and technical services	1.6	1.4	−12.5	0.01	0.2	1,007
Depository institutions	n/a	n/a	n/a	1.1	2.2	94.2
Real estate and rental and leasing	n/a	n/a	n/a	0.2	0.4	105.2

Source: US Bureau of Economic Analysis.

employed 45,000 people, paying more than US$4.1 billion in wages. The southeastern United States has been among the primary beneficiaries of Korean investment.[22]

South-Korea-US Relations in Economic Regionalism

The rapid development of economic regionalism has raised the concern of a potential discrimination against American exports to Asia. Since 2000, Asia has become the United States' largest source of imports and second largest export market after the North America region. Hence, the United States' economic motivation for closer relations with the Asian region is for the exports of its goods and services, a vital factor for its economic future.[23] Politically, the United States considers China's

[22] "Korean Investment on the Rise; Southeast US Still a Prime Target", "*Global Atlanta*, 30 August 2016 <http://www.globalatlanta.com/korean-investment-rise-southeast-u-s-still-prime-target/> (accessed 26 September 2016).

[23] Mark E Manyin, et al., "Pivot to the Pacific? The Obama Administration's Rebalancing toward Asia", *CRS Report for Congress*, 28 March 2012.

rising economic importance and active involvement in regional affairs as a threat to America's dominance in the region. The regional economy led by China is likely to enhance China's influence in US-dominated global economic norms and institutions.

The KORUS FTA was signed when the United States began to launch its pivot to Asia against China's increasing influence. In July 2010, then Secretary of State Hillary Clinton declared US national interest in maintaining freedom of navigation in the South China Sea. After the strategic rebalancing policy to the Asia-Pacific was announced in fall 2011, the United States has initiated a series of moves, including new troop rotations to Australia, naval deployments in Singapore, military engagement with the Philippines and enhancing relations with India, Indonesia and Vietnam, beyond the multilateral economic arrangement.[24] Economically, the United States' active promotion of the TPP was widely perceived as a counterbalance to China's greater assertiveness in regional affairs. TPP represented the economic dimension of the United States' "pivot to Asia" policy. The United States aimed to maintain its dominance in the region amidst China's power emergence on both the military and diplomatic fronts. In President Obama's words, his (pivot to Asia) policy goal is to ensure that "the United States will play a larger and long-term role in shaping this region (the Asia-Pacific) and its future".[25]

KORUS FTA might have raised other Asian peers' interest in negotiating similar trade pacts with the United States or join the US-led TPP, in particular, Japan and Taiwan share many similar export items to US market with Korea. After Japan joined TPP in 2013, Thailand, the Philippines and Taiwan also expressed their deep interest in being a part of TPP. Unlike other Asian countries, it is not difficult for South Korea to participate in the TPP as US-South Korea FTA is already in force. South Korea has also signed bilateral FTAs with some TPP

---

[24] Susan V Lawrence, "US-China Relations: An Overview of Policy Issues", *CRS Report for Congress,* 1 August 2013.
[25] Mark E Manyin, et al., "Pivot to the Pacific? The Obama Administration's Rebalancing toward Asia", p. 1.

members, including Singapore, Chile and Peru. With other TPP members, such as Canada, Mexico, Vietnam and Japan, the bilateral FTAs are under negotiations. The greater the number of FTAs with TPP countries, the easier it is for South Korea to take part in the TPP. The potential enlargement of TPP boosted by the KORUS FTA might add pressure to other multilateral economic agreements, such as China-Japan-South Korea trilateral FTA and RCEP. As Japan and South Korea were aligned with the United States through FTA and TPP, China may want to push RCEP or the trilateral FTA to strengthen its role in Asia.

While the KORUS FTA would affect the development of economic regionalism in the Asia-Pacific, the intensifying institutional economic network in the region would influence South Korea's FTA with other countries as well. The smooth development of multilateral FTA like RCEP and TPP provides a platform for South Korea to proceed with trade talks with other countries. For example, Japan-South Korea FTA and China-Japan-South Korea FTA negotiations have largely been stalled because of Korean resentment towards Japan (eg. Japan's military invasion during WWII, Japanese politicians' visits to the Yasukuni Shrine and Japanese inadequate compensation for Chinese and Korean comfort women) and unsettled territory disputes over Liancourt Rocks (or Dokdo in Korean) between Japan and South Korea. With the RCEP and TPP, political relations between the two have greater likelihood of stabilising, thus smoothing the development of South Korea's FTA with Japan. Good relations between countries in East Asia are also beneficial for integrating North Korea into the regional economy in the future.

Conclusion

The KORUS FTA, which took effect in 2012, covers a wide range of trade and investment issues. The United States seeks to have greater access to the Korean market for its agricultural goods, automobiles and services. For South Korean leaders, the KORUS FTA is an important part of South Korea's road map for expanding its worldwide FTA net-work. It is also a key mechanism to promote reforms in the domestic economy and attract investments from the United States in the form of "inward technology transfer", aside from the increased access to the US market. The two countries could also look forward to a more solid US-South Korea security alliance through the bilateral FTA. It is expected that the trade deal could serve as an economic highway linking the US economy to East Asia's growing regionalism. The high quality KORUS could also define new "rules of the game" for other Asian countries to follow in the future.

Four years after the KORUS FTA has taken effect, bilateral trade and investment have attained clear development. South Korea's merchandise trade surplus with the United States has grown rapidly while its deficit in services has expanded. South Korea hopes to encourage more inward FDI from the United States through the bilateral FTA. Although this has been achieved, it also witnessed a jump in Korean investment in the United States. From the perspective of regional economic integration, the KORUS FTA is a catalyst for other Asian countries to establish institutionalised economic relations with the United States. It would also increase South Korea's bargaining leverage in pursuing FTAs with other countries. Simply put, the KORUS FTA serves important foreign policy interests for the two countries. It can be viewed as the country's response to challenges to its national security and geopolitical interest.

It is still too premature to arrive at a conclusion as to the ultimate impact of KORUS on the two countries and on the regional economy as a whole. With the likely proliferation of bilateral FTAs and multilateral FTAs, the KORUS FTA on South Korea may lose its effect in the long run. This is particularly so as how the institutionalised economic network in Asia-Pacific region will be developed is still a big question mark. China's emergence and active involvement in economic regionalism is considered as a threat to US dominance in the Asia-Pacific region Given the North Korea problem, uncertain relations across the Taiwan Strait and unresolved territorial disputes in the South China Sea, the United States could possibly see forging an economic alliance without China as a way to keep China in check. In a nutshell, the eventual effect of the KORUS FTA on South Korea's economic development depends on not only the opening up measures but also how economic regionalism will be developed eventually.

Chapter 4

South Korea's Free Trade Agreement with China

On 20 December 2015, a FTA between the People's Republic of China (PRC) and the ROK took effect, a milestone in bilateral economic relations after the two countries established diplomatic relations in 1992. According to the FTA, 92% of South Korea's export items and 93% of China's will enjoy zero tariffs in bilateral trade in 20 years. Nonetheless, several items are excluded, including automobile, petrochemical products and rice. The slow pace of full implementation and the limited width of tariff cut suggest that bilateral trade in goods is not key to this bilateral FTA. Indeed, the two countries have sought to expand economic cooperation beyond traditional processing trade through this FTA. A follow-up negotiation on investment and services in 2017 or 2018 may promote greater economic opening up between the two countries.

This chapter will discuss South Korea-China FTA and its potential economic benefits and impact on both countries. It will review the bilateral relations in terms of trade and investment over the last two decades; the evolution of bilateral FTA proceeding with a discussion on its main text and tariff reduction schedule; the potential impact on bilateral goods and investment; and some geopolitical considerations behind the bilateral FTA. The conclusion will reiterate the main points raised in this chapter.

Lack of FTA Despite Close Economic Ties

According to South Korean official estimates, the FTA with China will raise its GDP growth by an additional 0.96 percentage point and create 53,800 new jobs in 10 years. In comparison, China's GDP will grow by an additional 0.34 point as a result of the FTA.[1] South Korea's greater dependence on China's economy is why the South Korean economy is the main beneficiary of the FTA. In 2014 for example, China was Korea's largest market. The share of exports to China in Korea's total exports (25%) was even larger than the combined exports to the United States and 28 countries in the EU (23%). In comparison, Korea only took 4% of China's total exports. Simply put, China's market is more important for Korean exporters than Korean market is for Chinese exporters. Apart from exports, Chinese products also took a large portion of Korea's total imports, accounting for 17% in 2014. In comparison, the share of Korean goods in China's total imports was 10%, the second largest in China, after the EU (Table 4-1). The FTA is supposed to give South Korea more competitive advantage vis-à-vis Japan and Taiwan in China's market. As a result of greater exports to than imports from China, South Korea ran a significant trade surplus vis-à-vis China from US$1.7 billion in 1995 to US$55 billion in 2014. The consistently growing trade surplus with China has also turned South Korea's overall trade into a surplus since 1998 except for during the global financial crisis in 2008.

The large exports to China have developed in tandem with Korea's massive outward investment in manufacturing sectors, especially in China's northeast region and Yellow Sea Rim over the last two decades. In the early 1990s, Korean companies venturing into China were mostly SMEs in the manufacturing of garment and textile, food processing and footwear. Beyond the low labour cost, proximity is another important consideration for most Korean manufacturers. From 1993

---

[1] "China-South Korea FTA Expected to Boost Chinese GDP", *Xinhua News*, 2 June 2015 <http://news.xinhuanet.com/english/video/2015-06/02/c_134291765.htm> (accessed 6 August 2015).

Table 4-1   China's and South Korea's Major Export Destinations and Import Origins in 2014

China's Major Trading Partners			
Top 5 Export Destinations	As % of China's Total Exports	Top 5 Import Origins	As % of China's Total Imports
USA	17	EU-28	12
EU-28	16	South Korea	10
Hong Kong	16	Japan	8
Japan	6	USA	8
South Korea	4	Taiwan	8
South Korea's Major Trading Partners			
Top 5 Export Destinations	As % of Korea's Total Exports	Top 5 Import Origins	As % of Korea's Total Imports
China	25	China	17
USA	12	EU-28	12
EU-28	9	Japan	10
Japan	6	USA	9
Hong Kong	5	Saudi Arabia	7

Source: World Trade Atlas.

to 2000, more than 85% of Korea's investment in China was in the northeast region (Heilongjiang, Jilan and Liaoning) and Yellow Sea Rim (Beijing, Hebei and Shandong).[2] After 2000, electronics and automobiles led mainly by Korean chaebols dominated the outward investment sectors. From SMEs to chaebols, Korean firms in China remained dependent on importing intermediate goods from South Korea for the final assembly. After China's accession to the WTO in 2001, the greater opening up of its market and more liberalisation measures for FDI generated another Korea's investment surge in China.

---

[2] Source of statistics: *China Foreign Investment Report 2011*, Ministry of Commerce of People's Republic of China (in Chinese).

China has been a particularly important overseas manufacturing production site for Korean manufacturers. Korea's outward investment in manufacturing soared from US$1.9 billion in 2002 to US$8.2 billion in 2007. During the same period, 47% to 65% of Korea's outward investment in manufacturing was in China, while its share in other Asian countries was around 16%-22%.[3] After the global financial crisis, China's wage hike was a huge factor for the continuous investment decline. Rising labour cost in China hurts Korean SMEs more than chaebols. To maintain their profitability, Korea's SMEs reallocate to Southeast Asian countries such as Vietnam and the Philippines where labour cost is relatively low.[4] Some Korean chaebols also moved factories to Southeast Asia while some choose to shift their manufacturing production to the inland cities of China where labour and operation costs are lower than those in the coastal cities. For example, Samsung has invested in Xi'an High-tech Industrial Development Zone to produce nanometre chips mainly for its smartphones and tablet PCs.[5] Unlike SMEs, Korean chaebols have the capacity to accommodate to China's policy shift from exports of manufactured goods to domestic demand. In recent years, they have adjusted their China strategies from a simple assembly location to become the "second Samsung", the "second LG", or the "second Hyundai" headquarters that encompass production, sales and R&D capacities.[6]

---

[3] Data source: Korea Exim Bank.

[4] "South Korean Enterprises Pursue Success in China", *Financial Times*, 9 September 2010, <http://www.ft.com/cms/s/2/82825ba0-bc02-11df-a972-00144feab49a. html#axzz2QsHj7i3Y> (accessed 17 April 2013); "Korean SMEs See PH as Overseas Investment Destination of Choice", *Asian Journal*, 27 December 2012 <http://www. asianjournal.com/dateline-philippines/headlines/18807-korean-smes-see-ph-as-overseas-investment-destination-of-choice-.html> (accessed 17 April 2013).

[5] "China-South Korea Pact First on Agenda", *Asia News Monitor*, 6 April 2012; "Samsung Launches US$7b Xi'an High Tech Factory", *China Internet Information Centre*, 13 September 2012, <http://www.china.org.cn/business/2012-09/13/content_26512600.htm> (accessed 16 April 2013).

[6] Zhan Xiaohong, "Analysis of South Korea's Direct Investment in China", *China & World Economy*, January/February 2005.

As a result of South Korea's massive investment, bilateral trade has developed quickly, particularly in ICT sectors. In 2012, 58% of Korea's total integrated circuit headed for China, including Hong Kong. Meanwhile, 59% of Korea's line telephones (eg. smartphones) and 66% of its computers and related components came from China.[7] The relatively large share of the ICT industry in Korean economy made its trade with China in ICT products vital. In 2012, 10% of Korea's GDP came from the ICT industry, up from 6% in 1992. Around 34% of its exports were for ICT related products.[8]

Nonetheless, subsequent to China's industrial upgrading after over 30 years of economic reforms, the bilateral trade based on Korea exporting intermediate goods to China for assembling final ICT products has changed. In 2004, the share of components and semi-finished goods imported from Korea among subsidiaries in China was 46.5% but this ratio declined to 19.2% in 2010. During the same period, China-based Korean firms' local procurement ratio increased from 38.6% to 64.7%.[9] The increasing share of local procurement in China showed that South Korea's technology lead over China has narrowed. According to the Korea Institute for Industrial Economics and Trade, the technology gap in the manufacturing industry had already narrowed to 3.7 years in 2011 on average, from 4.7 years in 2002.[10] Beyond China's industrial catching up, South Korea can no longer depend on exporting industrial goods to China for its economic growth given China's changing economic structure and economic slowdown. Hence, while South Korea is interested in China's huge market, it is

---

[7] HS Code for integrated circuit is 8542; HS code for line telephones is 8517 and HS code for computers and related components is 8471. Source: World Trade Atlas.

[8] Source of statistics: CEIC.

[9] Choi PilSoo, No Suyeon and Park Min Suk, "20 Years of the Korea-China Economic Relationship: Retrospect and Prospect", *KIEP World Economy Update*, vol. 2, no. 2, 15 October 2012, Korea Institute for International Economic Policy, p. 8.

[10] "China Rapidly Narrows Industrial Gap with Korea", *The China Post*, 18 August 2012, <http://www.chinapost.com.tw/business/asia/korea/2012/08/18/351320/China-rapidly.htm> (accessed 11 January 2012).

Table 4-2 Duty Free Products between China, Korea and Their Major Trading Partners in 2012

Destination Markets	Duty Free Products for China's Exporters		Duty Free Products for Korea's Exporters	
	As % of Total Product Items	As % of Total Product Value	As % of Total Product Items	As % of Total Product Value
Agricultural products				
Japan	35.9	27.4	18.9	19.0
EU	24.7	58.8	—	—
USA	26.6	54.1	30	18.4
Hong Kong	100.0	100.0	100.0	100.0
Korea	2.1	9.2	—	—
China	—	—	1.9	3.2
Non-agricultural products				
USA	45.7	63.5	46.3	64.2
EU	62.6	74.0	95.6	86.9
Hong Kong	100.0	100.0	100.0	100.0
Japan	68.8	76.4	54.0	67.1
Korea	14.1	32.4	—	—
China	—	—	9.5	43.3

Source: World Trade Organisation, China's trade profile, see <http://stat.wto.org/TariffProfiles/CN_e.htm>; Korea's trade profile, see <http://stat.wto.org/TariffProfiles/KR_e.htm> (accessed 14 July 2015).

concerned that more advanced industrial products from China could be making their way to Korea in the future.

Despite their close economic relations, compared with other trading partners, there are relatively fewer goods items traded freely between the two countries. In 2012, only 1.9% of Korean (3.2% in product value) and 2.1% of Chinese agricultural product items (9.2% in product value) enjoyed zero tariff in each other's market (Table 4-2). In terms of non-agricultural products, only 9.5% of products from Korea (43.3% in product value) and 14.1% from China (32.4% in product value) were traded without tariffs between the two countries (Table 4-2). Overall, Chinese products exported to Korea face tariff rates ranging from zero to 800.3%, while Korean products to China were levied at 0-65%. In consideration of the limited free trade items between China and Korea, the effect of FTA is expected to be significant on both countries' economy as over 90% of product items will be based on zero tariff. However, the slow path of implementation (in 20 years) narrow down the positive effect from the trade liberalization.

Slow in Tariff Cut and Diversified Measures in Korea-China FTA

The bilateral FTA began with a government-industry-university joint study in November 2006. The two countries conducted full study on issues such as trade in goods, trade in service and investment and potential impact on each other's industry and held five joint research meetings from 2006 to 2008. In 2010, the joint study in bilateral FTA was wrapped up. In May 2012, the China-ROK FTA negotiations were officially launched. After two-and-a-half years of talks, Chinese President Xi Jinping and South Korean President Park Geunhye announced the de facto conclusion of China-ROK FTA during the Asia-Pacific Economic Cooperation (APEC) summit in Beijing on 10 November 2014. In June 2015, the bilateral FTA was officially signed. The evolution of China-South Korea FTA is summarised in Table 4-3.

As shown in Table 4-4, the China-ROK FTA covers a wide range of measures to promote bilateral economic cooperation. It incorporates 22 chapters and seven annexes in total, covering not only trade in goods, trade in services and investment, but also a variety of regulatory frameworks such as competition policy, intellectual property right, dispute settlement, e-commerce, transparency and others for investment facilitation and further economic cooperation between the two countries.

Among the trade and investment facilitation measures, the most noticeable is the free trade schedule between the two countries. As

Table 4-3   Evolution of China-South Korea FTA

Follow-up negotiations

- 2017-2018
  (scheduled)

  The second phase of negotiation in service trade will be launched in two years after the implementation of the FTA

China-ROK FTA negotiations 2012-2015

- June 2015   China-ROK FTA officially signed (Seoul, South Korea)
- February 2015   China and South Korea completed the signing of all texts of the China-ROK FTA and confirmed the contents of the agreement
- November 2014   The heads of state of the two countries announced the conclusion of the substantive negotiations

Six times of negotiations in 2014

- November 2014   14th round of negotiations (Beijing, China)
- September 2014   13th round of negotiations (Beijing, China)
- July 2014   12th round of negotiations (Daegu, South Korea)
- May 2014   11th round of negotiations (Sichuan, China)
- March 2014   10th round of negotiations (Ilsan, South Korea)
- January 2014   9th round of negotiations (Xi'an, China)

Four times of negotiations in 2013

- November 2013   8th round of negotiations (Incheon, South Korea)
- September 2013   7th round of negotiations (Weifang, China)
- July 2013   6th round of negotiations (Busan, South Korea)
- April 2013   5th round of negotiations (Harbin, China)

Four times of negotiations in 2013

- October 2012   4th round of negotiations (Gyeongju, South Korea)
- August 2012   3rd round of negotiations (Weihai, China)
- July 2012   2nd round of negotiations (Jeju, South Korea)
- May 2012   Launch of China-ROK FTA negotiations (Beijing, China)

Joint Study on China-ROK FTA 2006–2010

- June 2010   Government-Industry-University Joint Study in FTA was wrapped up
- June 2008   5th round of the Joint Study Meeting (Beijing, China)
- February 2008   4th round of the Joint Study Meeting (Jeju, South Korea)
- October 2007   3rd round of the Joint Study Meeting (Weihai, China)
- July 2007   2nd round of the Joint Study Meeting (Seoul, South Korea)
- March 2007   1st round of the Joint Study Meeting (Beijing, China)
- November 2006   Both agreed to launch a joint feasibility study on the bilateral FTA

Source: Ministry of Foreign Affairs, Republic of South Korea, <http://www.mofat.go.kr/ENG/policy/fta/status/negotiation/china/index.jsp?menu=m_20_80_10&tabmenu=t_4&submenu=s_6> (accessed 11 November 2014); Ministry of Commerce, People's Republic of China, various online news.

Table 4-4   Summary of South Korea-China FTA Text

Preamble	**Both Parties Recognise Their Longstanding Friendship and Strong Economic and Trade Relationship and Desire to Strengthen Their Strategic Cooperative Partnership.**

22 Chapters

Chapter 1	Initial provisions and definitions
Chapter 2	National treatment and market access for goods
Chapter 3	Rules of origin and origin implementation procedures
Chapter 4	Customs procedures and trade facilitation
Chapter 5	Sanitary and phytosanitary measures
Chapter 6	Technical barriers to trade
Chapter 7	Trade remedies
Chapter 8	Trade in services
Chapter 9	Financial services
Chapter 10	Telecommunications
Chapter 11	Movement of natural persons
Chapter 12	Investment
Chapter 13	Electronic commerce
Chapter 14	Competition
Chapter 15	Intellectual property rights
Chapter 16	Environment and trade
Chapter 17	Economic cooperation
Chapter 18	Transparency
Chapter 19	Institutional provisions
Chapter 20	Dispute settlement
Chapter 21	Exceptions
Chapter 22	Final provision

7 Annexes

Annex 2-A	South Korea's schedule of tariff commitments
Annex 2-B	China's schedule of tariff commitments
Annex 3-A-Part II	Product rules of origins
Annex 8-A-1	South Korea's schedule of specific commitments
Annex 8-A-2	China's schedule of specific commitments
Annex 8-B	Co-production of films
Annex 8-C	Co-production of TV drama, documentary and animation for broadcasting purposes

Source: "Free Trade Agreement between the Government of the People's Republic of China and the Government of the Republic of Korea", China FTA Network, Ministry of Commerce, People's Republic of China <http://fta.mofcom.gov.cn/korea/korea_xdwb.shtml> (accessed 6 June 2015).

Table 4-5   Planned Tariff Reduction to Zero between South Korea and China

	China's Scheduled Tariff Reduction		South Korea's Scheduled Tariff Reduction	
	Product Items	Import Amounts	Product Items	Import Amounts
1. General items				
In 10 years				
Manufacturing products	72%	66%	90%	80%
Overall products	71%	66%	79%	77%
2. Sensitive items				
In 20 years				
Agricultural products	93%	56%	70%	40%
Manufacturing products	90%	85%	97%	94%
Overall products	**92%**	**91%**	**93%**	**95%**
3. Super-sensitive items				
Excluded from concessions	Autos, paraxylene, terephthalic acid and others		Rice, chilli, garlic, Chinese cabbage, apples, fisheries, livestock products and others	

Source: China FTA Network, Ministry of Commerce, People's Republic of China, <http://fta.mofcom.gov.cn/article/ftanews/201506/21870_1.html> (accessed 3 June 2015); Huh Moonjong, "Impact of the Korea-China FTA on the Korean Economy", *Issues briefs*, vol. 4, no. 45, 19 November 2014, Woori Finance Research Institute, <http://www.koreafocus.or.kr/design2/layout/content_print.asp?group_id=105671> (accessed 15 June 2015).

indicated in Table 4-5, products for tariff reduction are divided into three categories, including "general items, sensitive items and super-sensitive items". Products listed as "general items" will begin tariff reduction in 10 years whereas "sensitive items" will start tariff cut in 20 years and "super-sensitive items" will not be subject to tariff reduction. In 10 years, China will eliminate tariff for 72% of manufacturing products (or 66% of import amounts from South Korea) listed in the general items. In return, South Korea will reduce tariff for 90% of manufacturing products (or 80% of import amounts from China) listed in general items. In terms of sensitive items, China made more concession in agricultural items than South Korea did. In 20 years,

70% of Chinese agricultural goods will enjoy zero tariffs in the Korean market compared to 93% set by China for Korean agricultural goods. South Korea agrees to open relatively more for manufacturing imports (97% of import items) than China does (90%) in sensitive items. This shows that China allows a limited tariff reduction for Chinese agricultural products in South Korea's market in exchange for Chinese manufacturing goods' slightly greater access to the Korean market. While China is concerned about the potential impact on middle to high level manufacturing products (example, cars, machinery, chemical products, steel, electronic products, etc.), Korea is sensitive about cars and agricultural products. As such, both agreed to exclude the super-sensitive items, including some agricultural goods, automobile and some chemical products, from the tariff reduction. Overall, South Korea will completely eliminate its tariffs on 79% of all products imported from China within 10 years (77% of import amounts). On its part, China will remove tariffs on 71% of the products from South Korea over the same period (66% of import amounts). In 20 years, China and Korea will eliminate tariffs on 92% and 93% of trade items respectively.

Compared with Korea's FTA with other major economies, there are several differences with Korea-China FTA. First, its tariff reduction schedule with China took a much longer time to materialise. When Korea-US FTA was put into force on 25 March 2012, almost 80% of US exports of consumer and industrial products to Korea became duty free and nearly 95% of bilateral trade in consumer and industrial products will become duty free within five years. In the Korea-EU FTA, zero tariffs on 70% of machinery and appliance have been implemented since July 2011 when the FTA went into force. With India, the tariff reduction schedule is also relatively tighter than that of the China-Korea FTA. Since 2009, Korea and India have committed to zero tariff reduction in seven years for 90% of goods traded between the two countries.[11] On the FTA with ASEAN, tariff reduction schedule under

---

[11] "Korea-India CEPA", Korea Customs Service FTA Portal System, <http://www.customs.go.kr/kcshome/ main/content/ContentView.do?contentId=CONTENT_ID_000002362&layoutMenuNo=23270> (accessed 26 August 2015).

the Normal Track with six major countries in Southeast Asia has been set at 0% in five years starting from 2006.[12]

Second, South Korea opens less for Chinese agricultural products than it opens to other countries. South Korea opens only 40% of agriculture import values from China in 20 years. In comparison, the KORUS FTA eliminates tariffs on almost two-thirds (by value) of Korea's agriculture imports from the United States since the implementation of the agreement.[13] All EU agricultural products will have free access to the Korean market in 10 years after the implementation of the FTA.[14]

The slow path of opening (in 20 years) indicates that the benefits for both countries from the deal could be insignificant in the short term. On the other hand, this would help reduce potentially huge damages to farmers and industries from the two countries' trade liberalisation. Despite the slow implementation, the economic cooperation measures in the FTA provide both sides with the opportunity to further explore their business potential. For example, as indicated in the 17th chapter of the FTA, the economic cooperation covers agro-fisheries (example, food security, fisheries and forestry), industry (example, steel, ICT and textiles), energy and resource, science and technology, maritime transport, tourism, culture, pharmaceutical, medical devices and cosmetics. Advanced manufacturing, film and television production and health care for the elderly are among the sectors that the two countries are looking for complementary cooperation. China's enterprises can draw experiences from their Korean peers

---

[12] "ASEAN-Korea FTA", <http://akfta.asean.org/uploads/docs/agreements/AK-TIG-Annex1-Modality-2006.pdf> (accessed 26 August 2015).

[13] "US-Korea Free Trade Agreement", Office of the United States Trade Representative, <https://ustr.gov/trade-agreements/free-trade-agreements/korus-fta#> (accessed 29 June 2015).

[14] "EU-South Korea Free Trade Agreement: A Quick Reading Guide", European Commission, October 2010, <http://trade.ec.europa.eu/doclib/docs/2009/october/tradoc_145203.pdf> (accessed 1 July 2015).

whereas China's huge tourism and retail market will offer fresh opportunities for Korean companies.[15]

A total of 310 products manufactured in the Kaesong Industrial Complex (located in North Korea and run by South Korea) would be subject to preferential tariffs right after the FTA implementation. It is expected to allow more benefits for the inter-Korean industrial park than what other free trade pacts that South Korea has signed so far could offer.

To prevent unpredictable consequences after the FTA has been put into force, the "exception" in chapter 21 provides a "remedy". As stated in the final clause, "Where the Party is in serious balance of payments and external financial difficulties or threat thereof, it may, in accordance with the WTO Agreement and consistent with the Articles of *Agreement of the International Monetary Fund*, adopt measures deemed necessary".

Limited Short-Term Impact on Bilateral Trade in Goods

As mentioned in the previous section, 97% of manufacturing products listed in sensitive items from China will have zero tariffs in 20 years compared to 90% set by China for Korean goods. However, the advantages and potential impact on bilateral manufacturing trade could be overstated.

First, as shown in Table 4-6, ICT products accounted for the largest share in the bilateral trade relations. In 2014, ICT components were Korea's most important export items to China (19%) whereas China exported mainly final ICT products to Korea, including 20% of electrical apparatus for line telephony and 3% of automatic data processing machines and units. Both members of the Information Technology Agreement (ITA), China and South Korea have already removed the

---

[15] "China, ROK Sign Free Trade Agreement", China.org, 1 June 2015, <http://www.china.org.cn/world/2015-06/01/content_35710667.htm> (accessed 15 June 2015).

Table 4-6 Main Export Items between China and South Korea in 2014

South Korea's Main Exports to China		China's Main Exports to South Korea		
Product Items	As % of South Korea's Exports	Product Items	As % of China's Exports	Notes on Tariff
• Electronic integrated circuits and microassemblies (HS Code 8542)	15	• Electrical apparatus for line telephony (HS Code 8517)	20	• Based on ITA, no tariff on ICT goods
• Electrical apparatus for line telephony (HS Code 8517)	4	• Electronic integrated circuits and microassemblies (HS Code 8542)	5	
		• Automatic data processing machines and units (HS Code 8471)	3	
Subtotal	**19**	**Subtotal**	**28**	
• Liquid crystal devices (HS Code 9013)	11	• Liquid crystal devices (HS Code 9013)	3	• Tariff reduction in 10 years under FTA
• Cyclic hydrocarbons (HS Code 2902)	5	—		• Zero tariffs for most hydrocarbons items in the FTA
—		• Flat-rolled alloy steel (HS Code 7225)	2	• South Korea has set zero tariff for most steel products since 2004

Source: World Trade Atlas.

tariff on a variety of ICT goods (example, computer hardware and peripherals, telecommunications equipment, computer software, semiconductor manufacturing equipment, analytical instruments, and semiconductors and other electronic components).

Second, Liquid Crystal Devices (LCDs) are the second largest export products to each other's market. LCDs made in Korea are expected to benefit from tariff cuts in 10 years after the FTA goes into effect. However, as Chinese LCD makers are quickly catching up, the tariff reduction in a decade could be meaningless for Korean LCD makers to grasp China's market. For Chinese LCD makers, 10 years are long enough to grow the industry at home.

Third, petrochemical products are one of Korea's main export items. Except for hydrocarbons which are set to zero tariffs under the FTA, other petrochemical products such as paraxylene, terephthalic acid and ethylene glycol have been excluded from tariff concession.[16]

Fourth, China exports many steel products to Korea. Flat-rolled alloy steel accounted for 2% of total export to South Korea. Nonetheless, the FTA might not stimulate large imports of Chinese steel products since most imported steel products from 2004 under WTO rules have been set at zero tariffs.[17]

China excluded passenger cars from the negotiating table to protect its own automobile industry. However, the exclusion of automobiles[18] will not impact on Korean car makers as they now sell their locally produced cars in China without the need to export from Korea.

---

[16] "Korea-China FTA Opening New Chapter of Bilateral Economic Ties", *Business Korea*, vol. 31, no. 356, November 2014, pp. 23-24.

[17] "Korea-China FTA Opening New Chapter of Bilateral Economic Ties", *Business Korea*.

[18] Passenger cars were excluded from the negotiation table. However, South Korea will abolish tariffs on gasoline buses and trucks from China within 15 years of the implementation, while China will eliminate duties on buses and trucks from South Korea within 20 years. "Hyundai to Boost Localization after China-S. Korea FTA", *Want China Times*, 14 March 2015, <http://www.wantchinatimes.com/news-subclass-cnt.aspx?id=20150314000053&cid=1202> (accessed 8 June 2015).

As South Korea is aware of the growing insignificance of the traditional production network of Korea supplying intermediate goods to China for final assembly, the tariff reduction does not focus on intermediate goods for manufacturing production. Instead, Korean officials considered the bilateral FTA as a new channel for Korean SMEs exporting consumer goods (eg. clothing, leisure goods and high-end electronics) to the potentially huge market in China.[19] The tariff for some home appliances, chemical products for daily use (example, tooth paste, shampoo, shower gel, etc.) and Korean food stuff (example, dried laver, kimchi, etc) could enjoy zero tariffs in 10 to 20 years from the current 15%-25% tariff.[20] Nonetheless, these consumer goods do not account much in Korea's export to China even though it may benefit some Korean SMEs in manufacturing consumer goods.

For China, though it has prevented certain sensitive sectors (example, chemical and LCD industries) from Korean companies' immediate competition, the benefits for overall Chinese manufacturers will not be evident in the near term. It will take one decade for 90% of its manufacturing product items to enjoy free trade in the South Korean market, by which time, South Korea could have upgraded its industry even further.

Potential Boost in Bilateral Investment

Since China's economic opening up at the end of the 1970s, Korea has been one of the most important sources of FDI in China. In 2014, Korea invested US$3.97 billion in the country (Figure 4-1), making it the fifth largest foreign investor in China after Hong Kong (US$85.74 billion), Singapore (US$5.93 billion), Taiwan (US$5.18 billion) and Japan (US$4.33 billion).[21]

---

[19] "China, South Korea Reach Substantial Conclusion on FTA", Voice of America, 10 November 2014, <http://www.voanews.com/content/china-south-korea-reach-free-trade-agreement/2514313.html> (accessed 12 June 2015).

[20] "50 Inquiries about China-ROK FTA" (in Chinese), 2 June 2015.

[21] "News Release of National Assimilation of FDI from January to December 2014", Invest in China, 22 January 2015, <http://www.fdi.gov.cn/1800000121_33_4500_0_7.html> (accessed 27 June 2015).

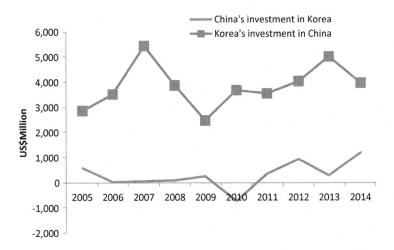

Figure 4-1   Bilateral Investment between South Korea and China 2005–2014

Source: 2013 Statistical Bulletin of China's Outward Foreign Direct Investment, China Statistics Press; South Korea Exim Bank, "Foreign Direct Investment Hits Record in 2014", 5 January 2015, <http://www.South Korea.net/NewsFocus/Policies/view?articleId=124506> (accessed 9 November 2015).

Korea's investment in China is mostly in the manufacturing sectors. Even with China's hike in labour wages in recent years, manufacturing investment still accounted for 81% of total Korean investment in China in 2014. In the same year, 19% of Korean investments were in the service sectors. Wholesale and retail trade and finance, insurance and real estate take the largest share of Korea's service investment in China (Figure 4-2).

Although China's ODI has drawn worldwide attention in recent years, its ODI in Korea is relatively less noteworthy. In 2013 for example, China made US$100 billion of investment abroad but only US$0.27 billion was in South Korea.[22] Nevertheless, compared with a few years ago, Chinese investment in Korea has increased. According to Korea's official figure, China invested US$1.19 billion in Korea in

---

[22] "Joint Report on Statistics of China's Outbound FDI 2013 Released", Ministry of Commerce, People's Republic of China, 12 September 2014, <http://english.mofcom.gov.cn/article/newsrelease/ significantnews/201409/20140900727958.shtml> (accessed 28 June 2015).

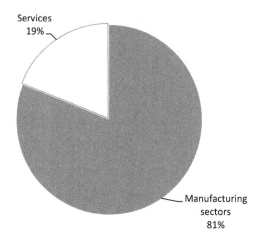

Figure 4-2   South Korea's FDI in China by Sector in 2014

Source: South Korea Eaim Bank.

2014, accounting for 6% of total FDI in the country. Despite the gradual improvement, the gap with Korean investment in China is still huge (Figure 4-2).

The FTA is expected to increase investment between the two countries as first, the two countries have agreed to open a variety of service sectors for mutual investment, covering several sub-sectors in business services, communication, construction, distribution, education, environment, financial services, tourism, recreational, cultural and sporting services and transport services (Table 4-7).

China has advanced opening measures for Korea in legal services, construction, environment and recreational, cultural and sporting services while Korea's opening for China's investment in courier services and construction is superior to its commitments to other countries so far. Chinese companies in courier services and construction are allowed to begin operation in Korea without setting up representative offices.[23]

---

[23] "Ministry of Commerce: China-ROK FTA Will Increase China's GDP by 0.34%", *China Daily*, 3 June 2015, <http://www.chinadaily.com.cn/micro-reading/china/2015-06-03/content_13788654.html> (accessed 15 July 2015).

Table 4-7   Specific Commitments in Services under China-ROK FTA

Sectors and Sub-sectors	China Opens to South Korea's Investment	South Korea Opens to China's Investment
1. Business services		
1.1 Professional services	V	V
1.2 Computer and related services	V	V
1.3 Research and development services		V
1.4 Real estate services	V	V
1.5 Rental/leasing services without operators		V
1.6 Other business services	V	V
2. Communication services		
2.1 Courier services	V	V
2.2 Telecommunication services		V
2.3 Value-added services	V	V
2.4 Audiovisual services	V	V
3. Construction services	V	V
4. Distribution services		
4.1 Commission agents' services	V	V
4.2 Wholesale trade services	V	V
4.3 Retailing services	V	V
4.4 Franchising services	V	V
5. Educational services		
5.1 Primary education services	V	
5.2 Secondary education services	V	
5.3 Higher education services	V	V
5.4 Adult education services	V	V
5.5 Other education services	V	
6. Environmental services		
6.1 Sewage services	V	V
6.2 Refuse disposal services	V	V
6.3 Clearing of exhaust gases services	V	

(*Continued*)

Table 4-7 (*Continued*)

Sectors and Sub-sectors	China Opens to South Korea's Investment	South Korea Opens to China's Investment
6.4 Noise abatement services	V	
6.5 Sanitation services	V	
6.6 Natural and landscape protection services	V	
6.7 Other environmental protection services	V	
7. Financial services		
7.1 Insurance and insurance related services	V	V
7.2 Banking and other financial services	V	V
8. Tourism and travel services		
8.1 Hotel and restaurants	V	V
8.2 Travel agencies and tour operators services	V	V
8.3 Tourist guides services		V
9. Recreational, cultural and sporting services		
9.1 Entertainment services	V	V
9.2 Sporting and other recreational services	V	
10. Transport services		
10.1 Maritime transport services	V	V
10.2 Air transport services	V	V
10.3 Retail transport services	V	V
10.4 Road transport services	V	V
10.5 Pipeline transport		V
10.6 Services auxiliary to all modes of transport	V	V
10.7 Other transport services		V

Source: "Free Trade Agreement between the Government of the People's Republic of China and the Government of the Republic of Korea", China FTA Network, Ministry of Commerce, People's Republic of China <http://fta.mofcom.gov.cn/korea/korea_xdwb.shtml> (accessed 6 June 2015).

Second, according to chapter 12 on investment, the "national treatment", "most-favoured-nation treatment", "access to court of justice" and "transparency" of each other's domestic laws and regulations are considered as providing favourable conditions for investment between the two countries. The enforcement of IPR in chapter 15, "transparency" in chapter 18 and "dispute settlement" in chapter 20 are especially important for Korean investors as they are safeguards for their business operation in China. In particular the IPR measure is expected to boost the Korean entertainment industry as Korean companies can have up to 49% stake in Chinese entertainment firms. China is an important market for Korean drama makers.[24] More joint production in cinema, TV dramas and broadcasting between the two countries is expected.

The bilateral FTA would also encourage investment in financial sectors and telecommunications between the two countries. This is also the first time that China includes "telecommunication" and "financial services" as separate chapters in the FTAs. China regards this as an initial step towards "high standard" FTAs with advanced countries in the future.[25] So is the inclusion of environment, electronic commerce and investment measures.[26] Although Koreans are concerned about the potential large presence of Chinese telecommunication business in Korea, the prospects of their financial institutions benefiting from greater access to China's financial market through the FTA could have more than offset the setback.[27]

The potential large investment between the two countries necessitates people's movement from the two sides to be fluid. China and

---

[24] "Culture Trade Balance: Cultural Exports to Surpass 1 Trillion Won This Year", Business Korea, 26 December 2014, <http://www.businesskorea.co.kr/article/8231/culture-trade-balance-cultural-exports-surpass-1-trillion-won-year> (accessed 15 July 2015).

[25] "50 Inquiries about China-ROK FTA" (in Chinese), 2 June 2015.

[26] "Key Point in China-Korea FTA: China Wants Something Different" (in Chinese), CommonWealth magazine.

[27] "Korea-China FTA Opening New Chapter of Bilateral Economic Ties", *Business Korea*.

South Korea agree to allow their citizens to apply for multiple entry visas provided that there is no criminal record on their first visit. For the internal dispatch in the same company, both Korean citizens and foreigners can enjoy two years of long-term residency in China. The same applies to the Chinese in South Korea.[28]

South Korea-China FTA in a Dynamic Regional Architecture

Compared with China, Korea is more active in FTA negotiations with both RCEP and TPP members. South Korea has concluded or is negotiating FTA with TPP members, such as Canada, Mexico, Japan and Vietnam whereas China does not have any bilateral FTA plan with these countries so far (Table 4-8). Unlike TPP, RCEP's "lower standard" in requirements has facilitated negotiation. Even with a positive outlook for RCEP, South Korea is still vigorously engaging in bilateral trade negotiations with different RCEP members. Korea's FTA with India is in effect and its FTA with Indonesia is proceeding while China does not have any FTA initiatives with these two countries.

From South Korea's perspective, as the country has FTAs with the United States and the EU, the FTA with China would put Korea in a central position in connecting the American, European and East Asian economies, thus benefiting it in the long term. Beyond economic considerations, the bilateral FTA is advantageous for South Korea geopolitically as a stronger relationship with Beijing could act as a buffer for Pyongyang's hostile policies towards Seoul. The Korea-US Alliance has been the linchpin to peace and stability on the Korean peninsula since the early 1950s. However, as closer China-ROK relations through the FTA provide another source of regional stability.

For China, the FTA with South Korea is essential as Korea is the most important FTA partner country for China in terms of population and GDP. Concluding a FTA with a relatively large country with an

---

[28] "50 Inquiries about China-ROK FTA" (in Chinese), 2 June 2015

Table 4-8   South Korea's and China's FTA with Other Economies in 2015

	China	South Korea
Current RCEP members		
ASEAN	E	E
India		E
South Korea	C	—
Indonesia		N
China	—	C
Current TPP members		
Chile	E	E
Peru	E	E
Canada		N
Mexico		N
Vietnam		N
Japan		N
Countries involved in both RCEP and TPP		
Australia	C	N
New Zealand	E	N
Singapore	E	E
Rest of the world		
EU		E
Free Trade Agreement between member states of the European Free Trade Association		E
Gulf Cooperation Council	N	N
Turkey		C
Colombia		C
Pakistan	E	
Hong Kong	E	
Macau	E	
Costa Rica	E	
Iceland	E	
Switzerland	E	
Norway	N	
Sri Lanka	N	

Source: Ministry of Commerce, PRC and Ministry of Foreign Affairs, ROK.
Note: 1. EFTA includes Iceland, Norway, Liechtenstein and Switzerland.
2. "E" refers to FTA in effect, "C" to FTA concluded and "N" to FTA under negotiation.
3. the United States withdrew from TPP in January 2017.

extensive FTA network is not only significant symbolically for China to advance its regional economic integration but also beneficial for Chinese business expansion. For example, Chinese companies can take advantage of Korea's FTAs with the EU and the United States to sell their products to these two markets. The inclusion of investment and services in this FTA shows China's capacity and willingness to conclude a "higher standard" agreement, a step nearer to the TPP or other FTAs with advanced countries.

The bilateral FTA also provides an impetus for China to promote regional economic integration by first allowing China to put pressure on Taiwan to accelerate the passage of cross-strait service trade agreement that has been stalled in the Taiwanese parliament since March 2014. As the spokesperson at China's Taiwan affairs office has remarked: "China-ROK FTA has undoubtedly challenged cross-strait economic cooperation.....As such, there is an urgency to finalise the follow-up ECFA negotiations".[29]

Second is by pressuring Japan to move towards the trilateral FTA given the importance of China and South Korea in Japan's external trade. The seventh round of negotiations on the trilateral FTA was held in Seoul from 12 to 13 May 2015. The progress on the trilateral FTA is expected to boost RCEP negotiations.

Third is by allowing Beijing to move closer to international standards on trade and investment given the "higher standard" requirement in this FTA; it will further open up China's market, reinforcing rather than undermining the current global economic system.[30]

Deeper cooperation between the two countries in regional affairs can be expected as both share common goals in regional development. Korea's Eurasia initiative is to link Europe and Asia by connecting

---

[29] "Taiwan Affairs Office: China-ROK FTA Made ECFA Follow up Negotiations More Urgent" (in Chinese), *People's Daily*, 26 November 2014, <http://tw.people.com.cn/n/2014/1126/c14657-26097025. html> (accessed 28 June 2015).

[30] Troy Stangarone, "Three Questions about the Korea-China FTA", Korea Economic Institute of America, <http://keia.org/three-questions-about-korea-china-fta> (accessed 29 June 2015).

transportation, logistics and trade and energy infrastructure networks across the Eurasian continent. For China, it plans to link Asia with Europe through the Silk Road Economic Belt and the 21st Century Maritime Silk Road (Belt and Road) initiatives.

Conclusion

Trade in manufactured goods with China has been an important source of Korea's GDP growth. Nonetheless, as China's economy is developing towards a more consumption one, South Korea can no longer depend on exporting intermediate goods to China for its economic growth. China's implementation of minimum wages since 2007 has already changed the production network with South Korea. The country is no longer a final assembly place for Korean investors. As such, for this FTA, the two countries are looking beyond traditional processing trade in which Korea exports intermediate goods for final assembly in China. Korea expects to gain greater access to the Chinese market for Korean consumer goods and service business with China's push for a consumption-based economy. For China, this FTA may allow it to advance manufacturing production and improve the quality of its services sectors through industrial cooperation with South Korea. The inclusion of investment and services in this FTA also shows that China is able to conclude a "higher standard" agreement.

Looking into the future, China's emerging market and proximity to South Korea will continue to provide business opportunities for Korean entrepreneurs. South Korea could also benefit by providing Chinese tourists with high quality services in, for instance the health-care sectors. The income generated from high value-added services would then help to enable domestic consumption. Beyond the service sectors, China is interested in Korea's high-end manufacturing industries for their more advanced technologies. The "made in Korea" branding and Korea's wider FTA network with both developing and developed countries are also attractive to Chinese investors.

Although the tariff reduction in merchandise trade is limited, the two sides have committed to cooperate in other areas to enhance bilateral trade and industrial integration. In particular, the inclusion of products manufactured in the Kaesong Industrial Complex in the FTA is expected to contribute to the growth and stability of the Korean peninsula. In the long term, the industrial cooperation and further liberalisation in investment and services are expected to enhance the connections between the two economies. Geopolitically, the FTA could also play a role in achieving the two countries' regional development goals by linking Korea's Eurasia initiatives with China's "One Belt, One Road" plan.

Chapter 5

South Korea's Income Inequality

Income inequality was not an issue for South Korea before the 1970s; the dramatic economic growth rates had kept the economy buoyant and the people employed. The turning point came after the country has begun to experience relatively higher inflationary rates and worsening income distribution since the 1970s. The oft-cited causes include the low interest policy, rapid development of urbanisation and large companies' dominance in business.[1] In recent years, South Korea's Gini index had clearly improved, dipping from 35.8 in 2000 to 30.2 in 2013 according to *The World Factbook*.[2] Although Korea's income inequality, measured by Gini index, is not particularly serious when compared to that of other countries, many Koreans felt the strains of an unfair distribution of economic gains.

This chapter will delve into the underlying reasons for South Korea's income inequality in recent years. The first section examines the different evaluation measures for South Korea's income inequality over the last two decades. Reasons for the development of South Korea's income inequality are outlined in the second to fourth sections, including the hollowing out of the manufacturing sectors, the limited employment created by profitable chaebols and labour market dualism. Some economic concerns

---

[1] Jong Goo Yoo, "Income Distribution in Korea", in Jene K Kwon (ed.), *Korea Economic Development*, 1990, Greenwood, Connecticut, pp. 372–391.

[2] Data source: *The World Factbook*, Central Intelligence Agency, <https://www.cia.gov/library/publications/the-world-factbook/fields/2172.html> (accessed 4 January 2016).

and political implications from the income inequality are discussed in the fourth section. Major findings and key points are summarised in the conclusion.

Measuring Korea's Rising Income Inequality

The yawning wealth gap between the rich and the poor in South Korea has become a concern for the government in recent years. Former Premier Chung Un-Chan had warned in 2011 that "this (gap between rich and poor) was a more serious matter than relations with North Korea".[3]

As shown in Figure 5-1, South Korea's income inequality measured by market income-based Gini coefficient[4] had increased progressively in the years following the Asian financial crisis to 0.298 in 1999, from 0.264 in 1997. It worsened after the global financial crisis in 2008, peaking at 0.320 in 2009 and slowing down to 0.307 in 2013. South Korea's Gini coefficient measured by disposable income shows relatively moderate growth from 0.257 in 1997 to 0.288 in 1999, 0.295 in 2009 and 0.28 in 2013. The enlarging gap between market income and disposable income-based Gini coefficient indicates that the Korean income redistribution policies through taxing the better paid might have been effective.

The relative poverty rate[5] based on market income also shows a surging trend from 8.7% in 1997 to 15.4% in 2009 and a slight decline to 14.5% in 2013. Similar to Gini coefficient, the relative poverty rate based on disposable income also had a mild growth from 8.7% in 1997 to 11.8% in 2013 (Figure 5-2). In absolute terms, the number was

---

[3] Ben McGrath "Social Inequality Worsening in South Korea", World Socialist website, 27 September 2011 <http://www.wsws.org/en/articles/2011/09/kore-s27.html> (accessed 21 November 2014).

[4] In Gini coefficient, "0" means everyone has the same income and "1" indicates one person owns all the income.

[5] Relative poverty rate is defined as the share of the population living on less than half of the median income. *OECD Economic Survey Korea*, April 2012, p. 17, <http://www.oecd.org/eco/501914 44.pdf> (accessed 10 November 2014).

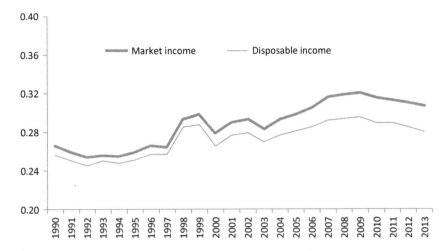

Figure 5-1 Gini Coefficient in South Korea for the urban household 1990–2013

Source: CEIC.

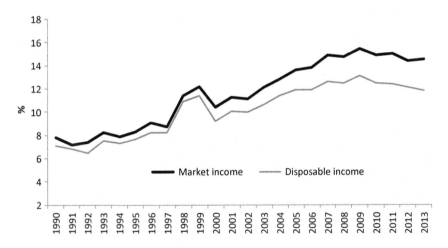

Figure 5-2 Relative Poverty Rate in South Korea 1990–2013

Source: CEIC.

more shocking. From 2011 to 2013, more than three million people fell into relative poverty with US$18,000 of annual income or less.[6]

---

[6]"Household Income", *The Korean Herald*, 8 December 2014, <http://www.korea-herald.com/ view.php?ud=20141208000572> (accessed 10 December 2014).

Income inequality and poverty are particularly serious among the elderly. According to Korean official statistics, in 2013, the Gini coefficient and the relative poverty rate for those aged 65 and above stood at 0.42% and 48% respectively, much higher than the national average ratio mentioned earlier. The official survey in 2014 also shows that 60% of Koreans between 55 and 79 years old were looking for jobs to meet living expenses.[7] The decline in family support and lack of proper public pension scheme are often cited as reasons behind the elderly poverty problem. Hence, a series of policies aimed at providing assistance to the elderly has been initiated. Although the Korean government has further put forward a multi-pillar system to financially support the elderly since 2008, the trend does not seem to suggest that the elderly poverty problem will improve anytime soon given its rapid ageing population (see Chapter 6 for more discussions on the financial vulnerabilities of South Korea's elders).[8]

Another way to assess income inequality is to look at the taxable income distribution. According to Korea's National Tax Service data, 71% of Korean taxpayers earned 20 million won (about US$18,255) or less in 2011. In comparison, only 0.8% of taxpayers earned 500 million won (about US$456,359) or more in the same year. The difference in the two income groups was as high as 25 times. Twenty-eight per cent of taxpayers came under the middle spectrum (subtotal of income groups 2, 3 and 4 in Table 5-1). In the same year, 95.4% of taxpayers made 56.4% of total taxable income (subtotal of income groups 1, 2 and 3 in Table 5-1), while another 43.6% of taxable income was made by only 4.6% of taxpayers (subtotal of income groups 4 and 5 in Table 5-1).

---

[7] "2014 Statistics on the Aged", Statistics Korea, <http://kostat.go.kr/portal/english/news/1/23/2/ index.board?bmode=read&bSeq=&aSeq=331389&pageNo=1&rowNum=10&navCount=10&currPg=&sTarget=title&sTxt=> (accessed 19 November 2014).

[8] Randall S Jones and Urasawa Satoshi, "Reducing Income Inequality and Poverty and Promoting Social Mobility in Korea", *OECD Economic Department Working Paper*, no. 1153, 2014, pp. 1-37.

Table 5-1   South Korea's Taxable Income Profile in 2011

By Income Group	As % of Total Taxpayers	As % of Total Taxable Income
Zero won or less	4.6	0
10 million won or less	45.2	8.5
20 million won or less	21.2	10.7
Sub-total (1)	**71.0**	**19.2**
40 million won or less	13.7	13.6
60 million won or less	5.6	9.7
Sub-total (2)	**19.3**	**23.3**
80 million won or less	3.2	7.9
100 million won or less	1.9	6.0
Sub-total (3)	**5.1**	**13.9**
200 million won or less	3.0	14.5
300 million won or less	0.7	6.3
Sub-total (4)	**3.8**	**20.8**
500 million won or less	0.5	6.1
1 billion won or less	0.2	5.9
1 billion won over	0.1	10.7
Sub-total (5)	**0.8**	**22.8**
Total	100	100

Source: Statistical Yearbook of National Tax 2012, National Tax Service, Republic of Korea, Table 3-1-4.
Note: The percentages are calculated by the author.

Although South Korea's income disparity has been gradually worsening over the past two decades (Figure 5-1), compared with the average Gini coefficient of 0.315 for OECD countries in 2011, South Korea's Gini coefficient was slightly lower (0.307) (Appendix 5-1). Measured by the Lorenz curve,[9] South Korea's income inequality (31.1) in 2011 was also less severe than that of most Asia-Pacific countries

---

[9] This index measures the degree of inequality in the distribution of family income in a country. Calculated based on the Lorenz curve, the cumulative family income is plotted against the number of families arranged from the poorest to the richest.

such as Malaysia, Singapore, Taiwan and Thailand. It was only slightly higher than the 30.6 in the EU in 2012 and better than some advanced countries, such as the United States in 2007, United Kingdom in 2012 and Canada in 2005 (Appendix 5-2). However, due to its oversimplification and exclusion of personal wealth from other sources,[10] it is often argued that the Gini coefficients may not provide an accurate picture of South Korea's income inequality problem. Moreover, the income inequality figures do not seem to match reality, suggesting a larger problem than what the figures can reflect. The investigation of social and economic changes in the recent decades in the following sections may provide a more comprehensive picture of the development of income inequality in South Korea.

Growing Export-Oriented Economy with Limited Job Supply in Manufacturing at Home

The growing share of manufacturing in GDP explains the Korean economy's quick rebound from the Asian financial crisis. However, the greater share does not translate to more employment in the manufacturing sectors; instead it has facilitated a shift of employment from manufacturing to low-skilled service jobs, thus enlarging the income dispersion.

As shown in Figure 5-3, South Korea's economic growth rebounded quickly from the Asian financial crisis to 11% in 1999 and 9% in 2000, from -6% in 1998. Since 2000, its economy has maintained moderate growth except for the 0.7% growth rate during the global financial crisis in 2009. Manufacturing exports had been key to sustaining

---

The World Factbook, <https://www.cia.gov/library/publications/the-world-factbook/fields/2172.html> (accessed 10 February 2015).

[10] "Measuring Inequality", The World Bank, <http://web.worldbank.org/WBSITE/EXTERNAL/ TOPICS/EXTPOVERTY/EXTPA/0, contentMDK:20238991~menuPK:492138~pagePK:148956~piPK:216618~theSitePK:430367,00.html>; and "Inequality in Latin America", <http://www.laits.utexas.edu/lawdem/unit03/reading2/Gini_definition.html> (accessed 10 November 2014).

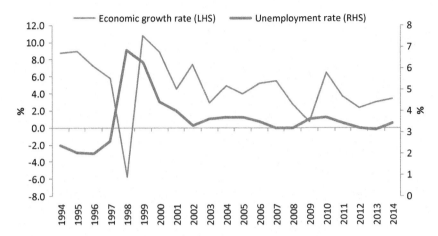

Figure 5-3 South Korea's Economic Growth Rate and Unemployment Rate, 1994–2014

Source: CEIC.

Korea's economic growth after the Asian financial crisis. Exports as a percentage of GDP increased from 32% in 1997 to 59% in 2013. Since 2000, between 85% and 90% of Korean exports have been manufacturing products.[11] China's growing importance in Korea's export has largely supported the country's post-crisis economic growth. Korean exports to China as a percentage of its total exports increased from 6% in 1996 to 26% in 2013. In 2013, a respective 43% and 33% of its exports to China and ASEAN were electrical machinery and machinery.[12]

Although South Korea registered robust GDP growth merely one year after the Asian financial crisis, the buoyant growth did not produce the corresponding jobs; unemployment rate remained high in 1998 (6.8%) and 1999 (6.3%). In the years that followed, there was slight improvement in the unemployment rate, declining to 4.4% in 2000 and hovering between 3.1% and 3.7% from 2002 to 2014.

---

[11] Data source: CEIC.

[12] Data source: World Trade Atlas.

Unemployment however could not attain the low 2–2.8% registered in the first half of the 1990s as indicated in Figure 5-3.

In terms of absolute numbers, the unemployed more than double from 556,500 in 1997 to peak at 1,463,400 in 1998. It slid to 1,353,000 in 1999, 752,000 in 2002 and remained quite stable (between 769,000 and 920,000) between 2003 and 2014. Although the number of unemployed has declined since 2003, it is still greater than the 410,000-549,000 between 1990 and 1996 before the crisis.[13]

The diverse development between manufacturing production and manufacturing employment is reflected in Figure 5-4. The manufacturing sectors have grown in terms of GDP share from 24% in 1997 to 31% in 2014, but the jobs generated dipped from 24% to 17% during the same period as a result of South Korea's massive outward investment in developing countries. Domestic industries began to focus on higher value-added production with fewer workers. Although the relocation of manufacturing production to other countries allowed Korea to upgrade domestic industries at home, the newly released high value-added work could not absorb all the laid-off workers from the manufacturing sectors. Other sectors had to take in the layoffs between 2004 and 2014; only 865,000 more workers found more lucrative jobs (items 1-5 in Table 5-2) while 2,551,000 had to content with lower paid jobs (items 7-16 in Table 5-2) compared to their counterparts in the manufacturing sectors. Overall, between 2004 and 2014, the service sectors took in 10 times more workers (2,551,000) at a lower pay than what the manufacturing sectors (261,000) had hired and triple that of sectors with wages higher than that of the manufacturing sectors. Health and social works had the highest growth in terms of the increased number of workers (1,105,000), followed by workers in business facilities and support services (463,000), membership organisations and repair and personal services (463,000). Among the sectors with wages higher than in manufacturing, the professional, scientific

---

[13] Data source: CEIC.

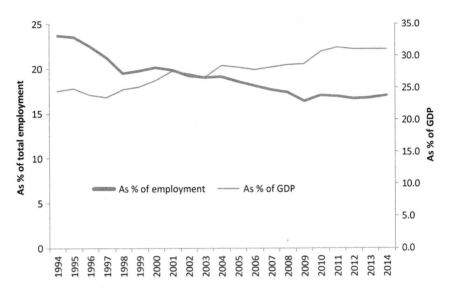

Figure 5-4 **Share of Manufacturing Sector in Employment and GDP 1994–2014**

Source: CEIC.

Table 5-2 Employment and Wages by Sector in 2004 and 2014

	A % of Total Employment		Increase (+) or Decrease (−) of Employment (1,000 persons)	Monthly Wages in 2014 (1,000 won)
	2004	2014		
1. Finance and insurance	3	3	+70	4,951
2. Electricity, gas and water supply	0.3	0.4	+19	4,598
3. Professional, scientific and technical	3	4	+415	4,498
4. Information and communication	3	3	+98	3,838
5. Education	7	7	+263	3,565

(*Continued*)

Table 5-2   (*Continued*)

	A % of Total Employment		Increase (+) or Decrease (−) of Employment (1,000 persons)	Monthly Wages in 2014 (1,000 won)
	2004	2014		
Sub-total 1–5	16	17	+865	—
6. Manufacturing	18	17	+261	3,447
7. Wholesale and retail trade	17	15	+70	3,178
8. Transportation	5	6	+244	2,892
9. Sewerage, recovery and remediation	0.2	0.3	+34	2,835
10. Health and social works	3	7	+1,105	2,678
11. Business facilities and support services	3	5	463	2,507
12. Real estate, renting and leasing	2	2	+45	2,254
13. Arts, sports and recreational	2	2	+51	2,303
14. Membership organisations, repair and personal services	5	5	+463	1,906
15. Construction	8	7	−3	1,838
16. Accommodation and food services	9	9	+79	1,759
Sub-total 7–16	54	58	+2,551	—
17. Agriculture, public administration and others	12	8	—	—

Source: CEIC.

and technical sectors received the highest increase in employment (415,000). In comparison, employment in high valued-added services such as financial and insurance registered relatively lower increase (70,000).

Chaebols' Growing Overseas Production Deteriorates Income Gap at Home

As mentioned in Chapter 2, Korean chaebols have been an important economic growth engine for the country. Their success in business has allowed them to offer better remuneration to their workers. Nonetheless, their contribution to domestic employment is limited. The expansion overseas in recent years has further reduced their demand for domestic workers who are mostly absorbed by the less profitable SMEs with lower wages.

Over the last two decades, Korea's large exports grew in tandem with its massive outward investment in the manufacturing sectors. Outward investment has been largely conducted by chaebols since 2000. Supplying intermediate goods to their overseas subsidiaries has been the main driving force behind Korea's rapid development in exports. Therefore, Korea's largest outward investment destinations are also its most important export markets, such as China and ASEAN.

Along with the expansion of outward investment in manufacturing was the growth in the share of overseas production in Korea's total output. The ratio of overseas plant production as total output at home and abroad surged from 6.7% in 2005 to 16.7% in 2010. Overseas production was especially large for ICT sectors. For example, overseas production of Korean smartphones swelled to over 80% of total smartphone production in 2013, from 16% in 2010.[14]

Relocating manufacturing sectors overseas allowed manufacturing companies to produce at lower cost and expand their profit. However, the majority of domestic workers did not benefit from chaebols' outward investment expansion. Chaebols' share of domestic employment fell from 18% in 1995 to 12% in 2010 according to OECD's

---

[14] "Growing Overseas Factory Production to Dampen S. Korea Economy", *Xinhua News*, 19 July 2012 <http://news.xinhuanet.com/english/business/2012-07/19/c_ 131725377.htm> (accessed 16 January 2015); and "Swelling Current Account Surplus Adds Pressure on Korea Won", Bloomberg, 28 August 2014, <http://www. bloomberg.com/news/2014-08-28/korea-s-current-account-surplus-adds-pressure-on-won.html> (accessed 16 January 2015).

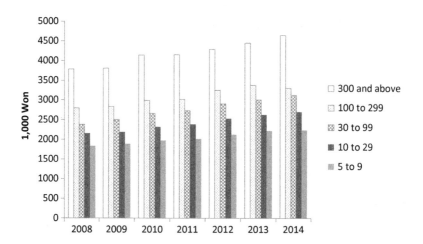

Figure 5-5 Korea's Monthly Wages by Number of Employees 2008–2014
Source: CEIC.

estimates[15] In 2013, 52% of the labour force was hired by companies with 5-299 employees and 39% of employment was in companies with 1-4 employees. Large companies with more than 300 employees accounted for only 9% of total employment.[16] Wage dispersion between large companies and SMEs with a bigger workforce has enlarged the income inequality. As shown in Figure 5-5, in 2014, the average monthly wage for workers of large companies (more than 300 employees) was 4,645,000 won (US$4,312), up from 3,787,000 won (US$3,516) in 2008. In comparison, the average monthly wage of workers in small companies (5-9 employees) increased from 1,834,000 won (US$1,527) in 2008 to 2,238,000 won (US$1,863) in 2014. Although monthly wages for workers in SMEs improved annually, the wage gap with large companies remains unchanged.

Labour Market Dualism Enlarges Wage Dispersion

Wage dispersion between regular and non-regular workers has been cited as another causal factor for the income disparity. Regular workers

---

[15] *OECD Economic Surveys Korea*, June 2014, p. 18.
[16] Data source: CEIC.

refer to those with a regular contract, better salary and better social protection than non-regular workers. Non-regular workers include temporary employees, family workers and daily rated workers. Non-regular workers were usually paid less than regular employees for the same job duties. The number of non-regular workers saw a clear rise after the Asian financial crisis.

As exhibited in Figure 5-6, between 1990 and 2013, regular and non-regular workers were the two largest working groups in South Korea, accounting for a respective 30% to 40% of total employment while self-employed workers accounted for less than a third. The development of regular and non-regular workers has changed over time. In the early 1990s, there were more non-regular workers than regular workers. Since 1992, the number of regular workers had slightly increased while non-regular workers decreased. Between 1992 and 1996, there was almost an equal number of regular and non-regular workers. After the Asian financial crisis, the number of non-regular workers grew to peak at 9,117,000 persons in 2002, from 7,644,000 before the crisis in 1996. In 2002, regular workers only numbered 6,862,000, a clear cut from 7,499,000 in 1996. Self-employed also registered a marked increase during the same period, from 5,710,000

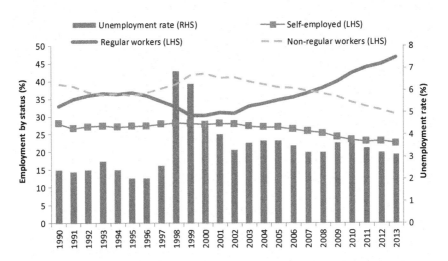

Figure 5-6   Employment by Working Status 1990–2013

Source: CEIC.

to 6,190,000. Non-regular workers constituted 42% of total employment in 1999, from 37% in 1996 while the share for regular workers
declined from 36% to 30% during the same period (Figure 5-6).

The Asian financial crisis triggered layoffs and early retirement,
pushing workers to move massively to self-employment and non-
regular jobs. As a result, the number of non-regular workers and
self-employed workers increased by 1.1 million and 0.29 million
respectively between 1998 and 2002 whereas the number of regular
workers decreased by 0.42 million. The "labour flexibility" policy
implemented by Democrat Kim Dae-jung after he came to office in
1998 further drove up the statistics for non-regular workers. This was
a condition set by the International Monetary Fund for a financial
bailout in the midst of the 1997-98 Asian financial crisis. The market-
based labour rules were supposedly directed at particular forms of
skilled labour. Nonetheless, companies increasingly took advantage of
the legalisation of temporary work agencies in 1998 and subcontract
work to work agencies to avoid the legal obligations.[17]

The measure saw an increase in non-regular workers and the gradual
improvement in unemployment rate in the years following the crisis.
Unemployment rate declined from 6.3% in 1999 to 3.6% in 2003.
During the same period, the share of non-regular workers maintained
at a high of between 40% and 42% whereas the share of regular workers
was between 30% and 33%. The self-employed lingered between 27%
and 28%.

Various measures have been taken to tackle labour market dualism,
the cause of income inequality. The 2007 labour law limited non-
regular workers' employment to a maximum of two years while supporting their transition to regular status. The law also prohibited
"unreasonable discrimination" in terms of wages and working conditions between regular and non-regular workers who work in the same

---

[17] Chang Dae-oup and Chae Jun-Ho, "Market Controls and Flexibility in Korea",
Asia Monitor Resource Centre, 27 September 2007, <http://www.amrc.org.hk/alu_
article/flexibility_of_labour/market_ controls_and_flexibility_in_korea> (accessed
21 November 2014).

or similar jobs.[18] However, some companies exploited loopholes that allowed them to dismiss their non-regular workers before the completion of their two years.[19] In 2011, the government launched the "Comprehensive Non-regular Workers Initiatives" to address the dualism problem by strengthening the social safety net and enhancing equal treatment for non-regular workers.[20] In 2013, the government announced another plan to convert around 26% of fixed-term workers in the public sector to regular status by 2015. Private firms were also encouraged to grant regular contracts to non-regular employees partly through tax incentives.[21]

With this policy, the number of non-regular workers with inferior wages and less protection from social insurance gradually decreased. As shown in Figure 5-6, before 2007, non-regular workers still outnumbered regular workers, but at a declining rate. Since 2008, the shares of regular workers have become consistently larger than that for non-regular workers. In 2013, 47% of those employed were regular workers, the highest since 1990 while non-regular workers and self-employed accounted for 31% and 23% respectively. The wage gap between regular and non-regular workers also narrowed. In July 2014, non-regular workers were paid 79% of the average monthly wage of regular workers. In comparison, in January 2008, the figure was only 41%.[22]

In spite of the improvement, Korea still has one of the highest percentages of insecure jobs compared to those of other advanced countries. Korean workers with job tenure of less than 12 months accounted for 31.8% of total employment in 2013, much higher than the 19.4% among OECD countries. The ratio for the youth in Korea aged between

---

[18] Randall S Jones and Urasawa Satoshi, "Reducing Income Inequality and Poverty and Promoting Social Mobility in Korea", p. 8.

[19] Ben McGrath, "Social Inequality Worsening in South Korea".

[20] Randall S Jones and Satoshi Urasawa, "Labour Market Policies to Promote Growth and Social Cohesion in Korea", *OECD Economic Department Working Papers*, no. 1068, 2013, p. 28.

[21] Randall S Jones and Urasawa Satoshi, "Reducing Income Inequality and Poverty and Promoting Social Mobility in Korea", p. 8.

[22] Data source: CEIC.

15 and 24 was particularly high (72.6%) compared to 26.8% for workers aged 25 to 54 and 36.6% for workers aged 55 to 64.[23]

Equity concerns are exacerbated by the low share of non-regular workers covered by social insurance. Although the number had decreased, there were still 7,703,000 non-regular workers in 2013, with a large majority not covered by social insurance. For example, in 2012, only 39% of non-regular workers were covered by the National Pension Scheme and 45% by the National Health Insurance scheme.[24] The conversion to regular status, however, does not guarantee permanent tenures. Over a 10-year period, 70% of workers who shifted from non-regular to regular status lost their regular status within four years.[25] Moreover, the greater shift of workers to regular status has taken a toll on the capacity of Korean companies, cutting out regular job opportunities for the fresh graduates.

Social and Economic Consequences of Growing Income Inequality

Despite the brilliant economic performance over the past few years, the sentiment among the general public in South Korea is not optimistic. The percentage of people who regarded themselves as "middle class" dropped from 55% in 2009 to 51% in 2013 compared to 61% in 1991. Fifty-eight per cent of Koreans viewed the likelihood of their socioeconomic status improving through hard work during their lifetime as slim.[26]

---

[23] Organisation for Economic Co-operation and Development, *OECD Employment Outlook 2014*, Paris, p. 279.

[24] Randall S Jones and Urasawa Satoshi, "Reducing Income Inequality and Poverty and Promoting Social Mobility in Korea", p. 7.

[25] Randall S Jones and Urasawa Satoshi, "Reducing Income Inequality and Poverty and Promoting Social Mobility in Korea", p. 8.

[26] "Fewer S. Koreans Consider Themselves Middle Class", *The Hankyoreh*, 6 December 2013, <http://english.hani.co.kr/arti/english_edition/e_national/614297.html> (accessed 10 November 2014).

The soaring prices for daily necessities have added frost to snow for the lower income groups. Official statistics showed that over the past few years, prices for food, clothing and housing registered the highest increase compared to that for other items. As daily expenses make up the bulk of the expenses of the low income groups, the soaring prices are a strain on their livelihood. As shown in Table 5-3, in 2014, people in the lowest quintile spent 18% of their income on food, beverages and tobacco while the highest quintile spent only 8%. The lowest quintile spent 13% of their income on housing, water, electricity and other fuels compared to 6% for the highest quintile. The lowest income household also spent more on health (9%) than the rich (4%). However, this is not to say that the high income earners spent less on daily necessities. They spent more in terms of absolute value because of the greater income base. However, the effect of the inflation of consumer goods on them was constrained by their possession of greater financial resources which provided a buffer for the higher food prices. It was the higher income group rather than the lowest income group who spent more on education, indicating that people born in poor families could have less access to higher education. Overall, the income of the lowest quintile was insufficient to cover their expenses in 2014 even with a large portion of transfer income (30%) from the government. As such, the lowest quintile registered income deficits of 140,000 won (US$127) whereas others were in surplus.

The lack of financial resources is an important reason for the growing household debt. In 2012, household debt was 1.6 times that of Koreans' annual disposable income, more than the average of 1.3 times for the OECD.[27] The government has taken a range of policy measures to address the problem. Ensuring sufficient credit and financial services to low income households is considered necessary to close the gap

---

[27] Randall S Jones and Kim Myungkyoo, "Addressing High Household Debt in Korea", *OECD Economic Department Working Papers*, no. 1164, 16 September 2014, pp. 1–37; and "Hold in Won", *The Economist*, 31 May 2014, <http://www.economist.com/news/finance-and-economics/21603047-korean-households-are-struggling-under-mounting-debt-hole-won> (accessed 10 December 2014).

Table 5-3 South Korea's Household Income and Expenditure by Income Quintile in 2014

	Lowest Quintile	Second Quintile	Third Quintile	Fourth Quintile	Highest Quintile
A. Disposable income (thousand won)	**1,115.1**	**2,311.9**	**3,113.7**	**4,072.3**	**6,284.7**
a. Regular income	96	99	98	98	95
1. Employee income	43	63	66	73	68
2. Self-employment income	22	24	22	18	21
3. Property income	1	1	0	0	1
4. Transfer income	30	11	10	7	5
b. Non-regular income	4	1	2	2	5
B. Household expenditure (thousand won)	**1,495.9**	**2,407.3**	**3,128.6**	**3,728.5**	**5,482.2**
a. Consumption expenditure (%)	84	81	78	76	71
1. Food, beverages and tobacco	*18*	*14*	*12*	*11*	*8*
2. Clothing and footwear	*4*	*5*	*6*	*6*	*5*
3. Housing, water, electricity and other fuels	*13*	*10*	*8*	*7*	*6*

4. Furnishing, household equipment and routine household maintenance	3	3	3	3	4
5. Health	9	5	5	5	4
6. Transport and communication	14	15	15	14	15
7. Recreation, culture, restaurants and hotels	13	15	15	16	14
8. *Education*	3	7	7	8	8
9. Miscellaneous goods and services	6	6	6	6	7
b. Non-consumption expenditure (%)	16	19	22	24	29
C. Surplus (B-A) (thousand won)	**−140.4**	**364.4**	**659.0**	**1,255.0**	**2,374.1**

Source: "Household Income and Expenditure Trends in the Second Quarter 2014", Statistics Korea.

between the rich and poor. One of the policy measures to alleviate the financial burden was to offer greater housing market credit for the low income. The government believes that if the low income households remain excluded from the financial market in terms of loans, they could not improve their economic conditions and income inequality would widen further.[28] However, the loosening of credit for housing could result in an upswing in housing prices which could further burden the low income group when purchasing a house. Skyrocketing housing prices may not hold for an ageing society like South Korea as the low birth rate will push down demand, resulting in lower housing prices in the future. Socially, the growing debt has often been linked to the high suicide rate.[29] Over the last two decades, suicide rate in South Korea increased noticeably from 7.6 for every 100,000 population in 1990, to 13.6 in 2000 and 31.2 in 2010.[30] In spite of the slight dip to 28.1 per 100,000 people in 2012, it was still remarkably higher than the average of OECD countries (12.1).[31]

To strengthen support for the low income group, government spending on social security had grown by 92.6 trillion won or 28% of total government spending in 2012 to 106 trillion won or 30% in 2014.[32] The progress however still compared poorly with that of other

---

[28] Randall S Jones and Kim Myungkyoo, "Addressing High Household Debt in Korea", p. 7.

[29] Christian Oliver and Song Jung-a, "South Korea: An Economy Divided", *Financial Times*, 29 May 2011.

[30] "2013 Social Survey", Statistics Korea, <file:///C:/Users/eaicmh/Downloads/2013ss(wspclicl).pdf> (accessed 27 October 2014).

[31] "Korea's Suicide Rate Remains Top in OECD", *The Korea Herald*, 2 July 2014, <http://www.koreaherald.com/view.php?ud=20140702001045> (accessed 19 December 2014).

[32] "2013 Budget Proposal", Press Release, Ministry of Strategy and Finance, 25 September 2012, <file:///C:/Users/eaicmh/Downloads/[MOSF%20Press%20Release]2013%20Budget%20Proposal.pdf> (accessed 10 December 2014); and "2015 Budget to Support Expansionary Fiscal Policies", Press Release, Ministry of Strategy and Finance, 18 September 2014 <http://english.mosf.go.kr/pre/view.do?bcd=N0001&seq=3688&bPage=1> (accessed 10 December 2014).

OECD countries. In 2012 for example, Korea's social spending was 9.3% of its GDP, less than half of the OECD average of 22%.[33] The low fertility rate and ageing population have also raised concern about the sustainability of government's increasing spending on social welfare. Creating more job opportunities is considered a more viable long-term solution to supporting the low income households. In June 2013, the government announced a road map to boost employment for 70% of its working population by 2017. Employment for both men and women is expected to increase to 78% and 62% respectively in 2017, from 75% and 54% in 2012.[34]

Income Inequality Generates Both Economic Concerns and Political Implications

According to the 2013 Social Survey, among those aged above 19, 49% was dissatisfied with their income. Only 13.6% of Koreans aged above 19 were satisfied with their overall life as a consumer.[35] Economically, insufficient income could dampen domestic consumption and economic growth prospects. Politically, the poor income also does not spell well for the ruling party's popularity. President Park Geun-hye's approval ratings slipped from its peak of 64% in April 2014 to 39.7% in December of the same year. So was the approval rating for the ruling Saenuri Party, which plummeted 3.7% to 38.9% during the same period. Beyond the income inequality issue, factors that contributed to the decline were the series of political scandals[36] and inefficiency in

---

[33] Randall S Jones and Urasawa Satoshi, "Reducing Income Inequality and Poverty and Promoting Social Mobility in Korea", p. 10.

[34] Randall S Jones and Urasawa Satoshi, "Reducing Income Inequality and Poverty and Promoting Social Mobility in Korea", p. 9.

[35] "2013 Social Survey", Statistics Korea.

[36] The political scandals include that of Lieutenant Choi who was being investigated for leaking an official document and subsequently committed suicide and President Park's younger brother who was also summoned by prosecutors. "Saenuri Scrambles as Park's Approval at Record Low", *Korea Joongang Daily*, 17 December 2014,

handling the Sewol ferry accident.[37] In April 2016, the governing party in South Korea lost the parliamentary majority it had held for 16 years. The disillusioned had cast their vote of no confidence with South Korea's sagging economy, including the unbalanced distribution of national wealth.

Indeed, the importance of income equity has not gone unnoticed by the South Korean government. South Korea's Finance Minister Choi Kyung-hwan has slapped a 10% tax on high-earning companies since 2014 unless the companies have spent a certain proportion of their income on dividends, investments and wages. This measure however was regarded by some as sapping the country's competitiveness as labour productivity has fallen since 2011. Forcing companies to spend their cash is also believed to have led to unproductive investment.[38] Thomas Piketty, author of the bestseller, *Capital in the Twenty-First Century*, posits that income inequality is a natural consequence of the capitalist system. In the South Korean case, the long-term dependence on export-oriented growth led by chaebols is a case in point.[39] The pressure to stay competitive in an increasingly competitive global market is one big hurdle for the government's push to equalise economic distribution.

<http://koreajoongangdaily.joins.com/news/article/article.aspx?aid=2998612&cloc=joongangdaily%7Chome%7C Cnewslist2> (accessed 19 December 2014).

[37] The Sewol sank on 16 April 2014 killing 304 people, mostly high school students who were on their way to a field trip to Jeju island, off South Korea's southern coast. Victims' families criticised the government for its cold response. Criticism also targeted the South Korean Coast Guard's ineffectiveness in carrying out the rescue operation. "Sewol Ferry Disaster: One Year on, Grieving Families Demand Answers", *CNN News*, 16 April 2015, <http://edition.cnn.com/2015/04/15/asia/sewol-ferry-korea-anniversary/> (accessed 12 August 2016).

[38] "South Korea's Confused Growth Plan", *The Wall Street Journal*, 3 November 2014 <http://online.wsj.com/articles/south-koreas-confused-growth-plan-1415060290> (accessed 5 December 2014); and "A Tempting Target", *The Economist*, 27 September 2014.

[39] "Piketty Discusses Distribution of Wealth in Korea", *Korea Joongang Daily*, 20 September 2014, <http://koreajoongangdaily.joins.com/news/article/Article.aspx?aid=2995112> (accessed 10 December 2014).

Economically, this strong dependence on exports to sustain economic growth is also risk-oriented. Though China's growing importance in Korea's manufacturing production contributed much to the country's post-crisis economic growth, such an economic growth cannot translate into job growth at home. Japanese yen's depreciation following Japan's monetary easing policy has also put much pressure on Korean exports in the global markets. In 2014, both Korea's finance minister and governor of BOK expressed their concern about the potential impact of the weak Japanese currency on Korea's economic prospect.[40] The uncertain export prospect renders the boosting of domestic consumption through equalising income imperative for maintaining healthy economic growth.

Income inequality however has not eroded the Korean people's faith in a capitalist economic system; the emphasis on national economic achievement (eg. high GDP growth, entry into OECD, G20, etc) rather than individual interest (eg. lower income in comparison with others) could be a contributor. The ambitious reforms such as progressive tax and welfare policies could play a part in reducing income inequality. However, to transform South Korea into a more equalised society, it will need strong social consensus. An income equalisation policy could not be achieved during Park's administration as it requires long-term efforts to bring it to fruition.

Conclusion

The Asian financial crisis in 1997 saw a worsening of income inequality in South Korea. Korea's market income-based Gini coefficient increased progressively from 0.264 in 1997 to 0.307 in 2013. The relative poverty rate based on market income also surged from 8.7% to 14.5% during the same period.

What gave rise to South Korea's income inequality could come from first, the de-industrialisation following the relocation of manufacturing

---

[40] "Bank of Korea Keeps Rate Unchanged as Lee Weighs Weak Yen", Bloomberg, 12 November 2014, <http://www.businessweek.com/news/2014-11-12/bank-of-korea-keeps-rate-unchanged-as-lee-weighs-weak-yen> (accessed 16 January 2015).

production to other countries. China's growing importance in Korea's manufacturing production contributed much to the country's post-crisis economic growth, but not to job growth at home. While the manufacturing sectors remain a bright spark in its GDP, from 27% in 2003 to 31% in 2014, the same cannot be said of its share in domestic employment which saw a downward slip from 24% to 17%.

Second, Korean chaebols' vast economic gains as a consequence of the relocation of their manufacturing plants to China were not shared by the majority of domestic workers. In 2013, 91% of Korean workers were hired by companies with less than 299 employees compared to the 9% in large companies with more than 300 employees.

Third, the massive layoffs and the "labour flexibility" policy set by the International Monetary Fund after the Asian financial crisis caused an expansion of poorly paid non-regular workers. While contributing to the country's employment rate (unemployment dipped from 6.8% in 1998 to 3.3% in 2002), these non-regular workers were paid less than regular workers and with less protection from social insurance.

President Park pledged to rebuild the middle class as part of her 2012 campaign, an effective political strategy that had greatly boosted her election chances. Dim economic prospects however have led her to introduce pro-large business measures and policies to promote economic growth after her assumption of office in 2013. Some scholars are calling for a stronger progressive tax, welfare expansion and policies for restructuring the economy. Nevertheless, income inequality requires long-term efforts and stronger societal consensus in support of these policies.

Appendix 5-1 Gini Coefficient in OECD Countries in 2011

Country	Gini Coefficient
Australia	0.324
Austria	0.282
Belgium	0.264 (2010)
Canada	0.316
Chile	0.503
Czech Republic	0.256
Denmark	0.253
Estonia	0.323
Finland	0.261
France	0.309
Germany	0.293
Greece	0.335
Hungary	0.290
Iceland	0.251
Ireland	0.302
Israel	0.377
Italy	0.321
Japan	0.336 (2010)
Korea	0.307
Luxembourg	0.276
Mexico	0.482
Netherlands	0.278
New Zealand	0.323
Norway	0.250
Poland	0.304
Portugal	0.341
Slovak Republic	0.261
Slovenia	0.245
Spain	0.344
Sweden	0.273

(*Continued*)

Appendix 5-1 (*Continued*)

Country	Gini Coefficient
Switzerland	0.289
Turkey	0.412
United Kingdom	0.344
United States	0.389
OECD	0.315

Source: "Rising Inequality: Youth and Poor Fall Further Behind", *Income Inequality Update*, OECD, June 2014, <www.oecd.org/els/soc/OECD2014-Income-Inequality-Update.pdf> (accessed 6 November 2014).

Appendix 5-2 Distribution of Family Income-Gini Index by Selected Countries/Regions

Country/Region	Distribution of Family Income	Country/Region	Distribution of Family Income
Asia-Pacific		**Europe**	
Australia	30.3 (2008)	European Union	30.6 (2012)
China	47.3 (2013)	Finland	26.8 (2008)
Hong Kong	53.7 (2011)	France	30.6 (2011)
Indonesia	36.8 (2009)	Germany	27.0 (2006)
Japan	37.6 (2008)	Greece	34.3 (2012)
South Korea	*31.1 (2011)*	Italy	31.9 (2012)
Macau	35.0 (2013)	Norway	25.0 (2008)
Malaysia	46.2 (2009)	Switzerland	28.7 (2012)
Philippines	44.8 (2009)	UK	32.3 (2012)
Singapore	46.3 (2013)	**North America**	
Thailand	39.4 (2010)	Canada	32.1 (2005)
Taiwan	34.2 (2011)	United States	45.0 (2007)

(*Continued*)

Appendix 5-2 (*Continued*)

Country/Region	Distribution of Family Income	Country/Region	Distribution of Family Income
Middle East, Africa and others		**South America**	
Bangladesh	32.1 (2010)	Brazil	51.9 (2012)
Egypt	30.8 (2008)	Colombia	55.9 (2010)
Israel	37.6 (2012)	Costa Rica	50.3 (2009)
Iran	44.5 (2006)	Ecuador	48.5 (2013)
India	36.8 (2004)	Mexico	48.3 (2008)
Russia	42.0 (2012)	Peru	48.1 (2010)
Turkey	40.2 (2010)	Venezuela	39.0 (2011)

Source: *The World Factbook*, <https://www.cia.gov/library/publications/the-world-factbook/fields/2172.html> (accessed 10 February 2015).

Note: This index measures the degree of inequality in the distribution of family income in a country, calculated from the Lorenz curve. The more equal a country's income distribution is, the lower its Gini index. If income has been distributed with perfect equality, the index would be zero. If income has been distributed with perfect inequality, the index would be 100.

Chapter 6

South Korea's Ageing Demography and its Challenges

South Korea is expected to become a "super-aged society" with over 20% of its population aged 65 years and older in 2026, just 10 years from 2016.[1] Falling total fertility rate (TFR) and rising longevity are the two fundamental contributors to the country's growing ageing population. The impact of an ageing demography on the country's labour force structure could be felt especially in recent years. The economic growth prospect may take a beating as saving, consumption and investment are expected to decline subsequent to the ageing demography. More importantly, an ageing population means a smaller workforce and therefore less tax revenue for the government to support the unemployed elderly. Indeed, since its post-war economic take-off, the Korean government has done relatively little in fostering a secure social safety for its senior citizens. As a dramatic change in demography

---

[1] "Super-aged" society is defined by the United Nations as one in which the elderly aged 65 and older make up at least 20% of the total population. "Ageing society" is defined as seniors aged 65 and older who account for at least 7% of total population and "aged society" is defined as a population with at least 14% in this age group. Neil Howe, Richard Jackson and Keisuke Nakashima, *The Ageing of Korea*, Centre for Strategic and International Studies, March 2007, p. 3, <http://csis.org/files/media/csis/pubs/070321_gai_agingkorea_eng.pdf> (accessed 28 March 2016); and Florence Lowe-Lee, "Is Korea Ready for the Demographic Revolution?" Korea Economic Institute of America, 2009, <http://www.keia.org/sites/default/files/publications/04Exchange09.pdf > (accessed 27 April 2016).

is expected in the coming decade, how to minimise the potential impact from an ageing society will unavoidably take top policy priority.

This chapter aims to examine South Korea's ageing demography and its potential impact on the economy. The first section gauges the significance of South Korea's ageing demography, current ageing population and population forecast relative to other countries in the world. The second reviews the evolution of South Korea's population. The main policy alternations and society changes have taken effect in various stages of population development over the last few decades. The third analyses South Korea's domestic employment by age group. Senior citizens have gradually taken dominance while young workers' share in domestic employment has been declining. The fourth examines the Korean elderly who is the most financially vulnerable group of people due to the inadequate pension system. Poverty among the elderly has become a critical social issue in recent years. The fifth addresses the government's policy response to the growing ageing population. The chapter concludes with a summary of the main points raised and the future challenges of an ageing demography.

South Korea's "Demographic Time Bomb"

With rising life expectancy and plummeting birthrates, South Korea is about to undergo a stunning demographic transformation. As shown in Table 6-1, in 2015, 18.5% of South Korea's total population was above 60 years old, still far below that of Japan and some European countries. However, South Korea's ageing population will grow very quickly in the coming decade. The ratio for people older than 60 years of age is expected to increase to 31.4% in 2030 and 41.5% in 2050, making it the third-oldest country in the world after Japan and Taiwan. In fact, South Korea has registered one of the fastest growth rates in terms of an ageing population, with 7.2% of growth rate for people over 60 years old between 2000 and 2015 and an estimated 12.7% between 2015 and 2030, behind only Cuba. According to the United Nations' forecast, the number of the elderly (aged 60 and older) in

Table 6-1   International Ranking of Estimated Percentage of Population Aged 60 and over in 2015, 2030 and 2050

Ranking	2015	2030	2050
1	Japan (33.1)	Martinique (38.5)	Taiwan (44.3)
2	Italy (28.6)	Japan (37.3)	Japan (42.5)
3	Germany (27.6)	Italy (36.6)	**South Korea (41.5)**
4	Finland (27.2)	Germany (36.1)	Spain (41.4)
5	Portugal (27.1)	Portugal (34.7)	Portugal (41.2)
15	Slovenia (25.2)	**South Korea (31.4)**	Austria (37.1)
53	**South Korea (18.5)**	China (25.3)	Réunion (30.9)

Source: *World Population Ageing 2015*, United Nations, 2015 <http://www.un.org/en/development/desa/population/publications/pdf/ageing/WPA2015_Report.pdf> (accessed 27 March 2016).

South Korea will increase from the current 9.4 million in 2015 to 16.8 million in 2030 and 21.0 million in 2044.[2]

The rapid decline of TFR explains the swift demographic ageing. Average TFR in South Korea had fallen quickly from 2.1 children per woman in 1983 to 1.3 between 2010 and 2015, only slightly higher than Hong Kong's 1.2, Thailand's 1.2, Taiwan's 1.1 and far below the global average of 2.5 (Table 6-2). The asymmetry is in the rapidly declining TFR and longer life expectancy. Life expectancy at birth in South Korea was 78 years old for male and 84.6 for female between 2010 and 2015, improving from 68 years old in 1985.[3] South Korea's life expectancy at birth is also clearly higher than the average of high-income, middle-income and low-income countries. As a consequence, the dependency ratio (measured by people aged 65 and older per 100 aged 20-64) is expected to increase from 50.6% in 2015 to 70.4% in 2030. Almost one South Korean will have to take care of one elderly aged above 65 in 2030, compared with two young Koreans to one elderly in 2015.

---

[2] *World Population Ageing 2015*, United Nations 2015.
[3] Howe, Jackson and Nakashima, *The Ageing of Korea*.

Table 6-2 Demographic Statistics of South Korea and the World

	Total Fertility Rate (Number of Children per Woman, 2010–2015)	Life Expectancy at Birth (2010–2015)		Total Dependency Ratio (%)		Labour Force Participation of Persons Aged 65 or over (2015) (%)	
		Male	Female	2015	2030	Male	Female
South Korea	**1.3**	**78.0**	**84.6**	**50.6**	**70.4**	**42.2**	**23.4**
High-income countries	1.7	75.7	81.9	64.8	78.0	18.2	9.8
Middle-income countries	2.4	67.7	71.5	70.8	71.0	35.3	15.9
Low-income countries	4.9	58.7	61.9	131.1	110.5	n/a	n/a
World average	2.5	68.3	72.7	73.5	75.7	30.2	14.4

Source: *World Population Ageing 2015*, United Nations 2015, <http://www.un.org/en/development/desa/population/publications/pdf/ageing/WPA2015_Report.pdf> (accessed 27 March 2016).

The limited growth of the young population would translate to lower growth in private consumption and national saving. The National Assembly Budget Office (NABO) in South Korea forecast that the changing demographics will drag down average economic growth from 3.8% in the 2014-2020 period to 2.6% in 2016-2030 and 1.7% in 2041-2045.[4] The labour force structure has been changing as well. Owing to the low TFR, the young labour force as a percentage of total labour force has quickly declined whereas the share of older workers has increased. The percentage of older workers in South Korea is particularly high (42.2% for male and 23.4% for female) compared with that of other countries (Table 6-2).

---

[4] Kim Eun-jung "Rapid Population Aging Impacts on S. Korean Job Market", *Yonhap News*, 19 February 2016, <http://english.yonhapnews.co.kr/feature/2016/02/18/65/0900000000AEN20160218000500320F.html> (accessed 28 March 2016).

An important reason for the high percentage of senior employment is the inadequate social welfare system for supporting the living expenses of the elderly. In 2014, 55% of the elderly aged 55–70 (about six million people) had neither private nor public pension to finance their daily necessities whereas 45% received an average pension of 490,000 won (about US$411.8) per month. South Korean seniors have traditionally relied on young family members to meet their financial demand. Due to the rise of "individualistic" or "western values", more and more South Koreans are convinced that their parents should support themselves. Hence, the demand for social welfare (eg. pension, health-care services) has been surging. Current government spending has not been able to meet the growing demand for pension of the elderly. The Centre for Strategic and International Studies estimated that the social welfare programme for the elderly, including long-term care, health care, pension and other welfare benefits in South Korea, can be increased from 2.6% of GDP in 2005 to 18.9% of GDP in 2050 assuming the current benefit programme remains unchanged.[5] Its relatively low government debt to GDP ratio (38%) indicates that South Korea is in a good financial position to provide greater welfare benefits to its elderly. Nevertheless, in the long run, the government's financial capabilities will diminish due to the shrinking working population. Maintaining moderate economic growth to support its expanding welfare programme will hence be a big challenge for the government.

Evolution of South Korea's Demographic Changes

Following the Korean War in the early 1950s, Korean society was chiefly rural and agricultural. Its TFR exceeded six children per woman. In 1960, its economy continued to remain one of the poorest in the world with US$79 of GDP per capita. The Korean government regarded the post-war baby boom and slow economic growth as making poverty a vicious cycle. As part of its economic development policies, the national family planning campaign to limit births began in

---

[5] Howe, Jackson and Nakashima, *The Ageing of Korea*, p. 15.

Figure 6-1   South Korea's GDP per Capita, Birth and Death Rate 1960–2015

Source: CEIC and Korean Statistical Information Service.

1962.[6] To further increase per capita living standard, the Park Chung-hee administration set out policies to reduce population growth, from a three-child family in 1968, to two-child family in 1971 and one or two-child in the early 1980s.[7] The family planning policy proved to be a success. As shown in Figure 6-1, the birth rates (number of newborn babies per 1,000 persons) declined from 44 in 1960 to 31 in 1970, 23 in 1980 and 15 in 1990. After the 2000s, the birth rate continued to fall to 8.6 in 2015.

Two decades after the post-war "baby boom", the economy began to benefit from the larger working population. Since 1990, the young working-age population (aged between 20 and 39) had surpassed the young population (0-19 years-old) to become the dominant group in South Korea's demography until 2009 (Figure 6-2). The "demographic dividend" (greater number of working population than young and elderly population) was evidenced by the significant growth of GDP per capita since the 1990s. South Korea's economy reached another

---

[6] Carl Haub, "Did South Korea's Population Policy Work Too Well?" Population Reference Bureau, 2010 <http://www.prb.org/Publications/Articles/2010/korea fertility.aspx> (accessed 18 April 2016).

[7] Howe, Jackson and Nakashima, *The Ageing of Korea*, p. 3.

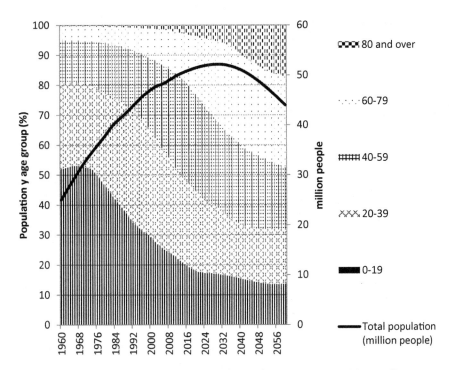

Figure 6-2   South Korea's Population by Age Group 1960–2060

Source: CEIC.

milestone after the 2000s as its GDP per capita peaked at US$27,214 in 2015, more than double that a decade ago.

However, the quick economic development is accompanied by the social trend of late marriages and childrearing.[8] The high cost of education and living is also reasons behind the low birth rate. The rapid slowing down of birth rate took place in tandem with the steady decline in death rate. Annual death rate dropped from 14 deaths per 1,000

---

[8] The average age for South Korean women's first marriage was 29 in 2013, from 24 in 1985. The chances of spinstership had risen from 9% in 2000 to 15% in 2013. "A Pram Too Far", *The Economist*, 26 October 2013, <http://www.economist.com/ news/special-report/21588207-faced-overwhelming-pressures-south-korean-women- have-gone-baby-strike-pram-too> (accessed 18 April 2016).

people in 1960 to five in 2015 due to improved public health measures and medical advances following economic development (Figure 6-1). As a result of the low birth rates and death rates, South Korea's demography has been changing. Between 1960 and 1976, there was 50% to 53% of total population aged below 19 years old in South Korea. However, this young population ratio halved (25%) in 2006 and down to 20% in 2015. Since 2017, the youth aged below 19 have been forecast to be less than 20% of the country's total population (Figure 6-2). People in the middle range (between 20 and 59 years old) reached their peak (62% of total population) between 2012 and 2014. Since 2015, the ratio has started to decline. By 2032, the middle age population is expected to be less than half of the total population. The elderly aged over 60 was only 5% of total population during the 1960-1979 period. The ratio had doubled to 10% since 1996 and tripled to 15% since 2009 and is estimated to reach 20% by 2017 and 30% by 2028. Hence, the "demographic dividend" is expected to end in 2048, overwhelmed by an ageing population. Overall, given the quick falling birth rates, total population is expected to drop from its peak of 52 million in 2028 to 44 million in 2058, with 30% to 47% aged above 65, according to the Korean government's projection.

In response, the Korean government has implemented several policies a few years ago. In 2005, an advisory committee to South Korea's president was formed and a law was passed to offer a legal framework to promote birth rates. The Saero-Maji Plan for the 2006-2010 period included measures to construct a favourable environment for childbearing. In 2006, the government announced "Vision 2020 Plan" to raise the TFR.[9] However, the policy initiatives have not been effective in boosting South Korea's TFR, which remains as one of the lowest in the world. The Korean government may have to rely on other labour policies to complement the current TFR promotion policy (eg. reduce working hours and encourage men to take leave to share childcare burden, etc). Society is seemingly not ready for this population structural change. For example, private companies may still need their

---

[9] Carl Haub, "Did South Korea's Population Policy Work Too Well?"

employees to work long hours and men may not be willing to share the childcare burden with women. Therefore, policies alone are not enough; enforcement also matters.

Ageing Population Changes Labour Force Structure

Population ageing has affected the structure of South Korea's labour force. As shown in Figure 6-3, over the last 15 years, the young labour force has been clearly declining whereas the number of senior workers has been rising. In 2000, South Korean workers aged between 15 and 29 accounted for 24% of the total labour force; this ratio however declined to 16% in 2015. During the same period, the share of workers aged between 30 and 44 also decreased from 43% to 34%. There was significant growth of senior workers to 36% in 2015 from 24% in 2000 for those between 45 and 59 years of age. The share of Korean workers above 60 years old increased from 9% to 14% during the same period. Although the total number of workers increased from 22 million in 2000 to 27 million in 2015, a downward trend is likely after its total

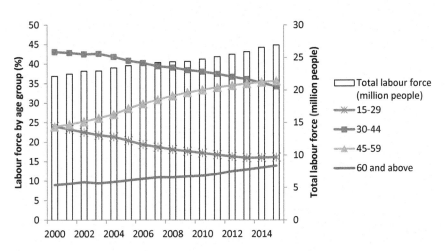

Figure 6-3   South Korea's Labour Force by Age Group 2000–2015
Source: CEIC.

population peaks in 2030. OECD estimated that over the period 2020–2050, the growth of workers in South Korea will become negative and experience a sharp drop.[10]

Two principal measures are imperative to counterbalance the potential impact on the economy from a shrinkage in the working population. First is to increase labour productivity. Since the economically active population will continue to age and lessen in numbers, productivity must be enhanced in order to maintain a decent level of economic rate. In 2014, South Korea's productivity was US$31.2 per hour worked, lower than OECD countries' average of US$45.9.[11] South Korea's low productivity is particularly obvious in services. OECD's figures show that South Korea's productivity in services in 2012 was only about 45% that of manufacturing sectors, far below OECD countries' average of 86%.[12] South Korea's low productivity in services can be attributed to the export-led growth strategy after the war which has attracted the most productive resources into manufacturing, instead of the large number of SMEs in services. Therefore, the service sectors have produced low profit margin and low value-added services. As services are gaining in importance in the economy after the relocation of manufacturing overseas, enhancing service sectors' productivity is critical for the country's future economic growth.

Second is the quantitative expansion of the labour force through the participation of women, the elderly, foreign workers and the young. Except for women aged between 35 and 44, women's labour participation rate in South Korea has improved over the last decade (Table 6-3). This shows that childbearing responsibility is still on the women when

---

[10] Phang Hanam S, "Demographic Dividend and Labour Force Transformation in Asia: The Case of the Republic of Korea", Proceedings of the United Nations Expert Group Meeting on Social and Economic Implications of Changing Population Age Structures, 31 August-2 September 2005, United Nations, <http://www.un.org/esa/population/meetings/Proceedings_EGM_Mex_2005/phang.pdf> (accessed 27 April 2016).

[11] OECD statistics.

[12] *OECD Economic Survey Korea*, June 2014, p. 18.

Table 6-3   Labour Statistics in South Korea and OECD Countries

	South Korea		OECD Average
	2000	2014	2014
1. Productivity (US$ per hour worked)	18.4	31.2	45.9
2. Female labour force participation rate by age group (%)			
25–29	56	73	72
30–34	49	60	71
35–39	**59**	**57**	**72**
40–44	**64**	**64**	**73**
45–49	65	70	74
50–54	55	66	71
55–59	51	58	62
3. Elderly labour force participation rate by age group (%)			
65–69	43	46	25
70–74	**27**	**34**	**15**
4. Unemployment rate by age group (%)			
15–24	11	10	15
25–34	5	6	9
35–44	3	2	6
45–54	3	2	6

Source: OECD Statistics.

they start a family. Unlike South Korea, women's labour participation rate remains relatively unchanged among different age groups in OECD countries' average. The inadequate childcare facilities and services could be a factor for the low labour participation rate for women in the 35-44 age group in South Korea. Wage dispersion may also have discouraged women participation in the workforce after marriage. In 2011, wages for female employees in South Korea were only 64% that of male employees, the largest gap among OECD countries.[13]

---

[13] *OECD Economic Surveys Korea*, June 2014, p. 24.

Unlike female employment, the elderly in South Korea not only constitutes a strong force, but also outstrips OECD countries' average. Participation rate for those aged between 70 and 74 had clear growth from 27% in 2000 to 34% in 2014, and double OECD countries' average of 15% (Table 6-3). The employment of foreign workers is also significant. According to official statistics for 2015, there were around 0.94 million foreign workers in South Korea, 91% of whom came from Asia. Nevertheless, the employment of foreign workers poses social integration problems to the host country.[14] Young unemployment rate remains high in South Korea. In March 2016, the unemployment rates for the 15-19 and 20-29 age cohorts were 14.6% and 11.6%, respectively. The lack of full-time positions among young workers is often considered as the main reason for the high youth unemployment rate.[15] The government is also seeking high technology to complement the shortage of labour. In 2014 there were 478 robots per 10,000 workers. The country plans to have one robotic device in every household by 2020 to help ease the burden of elderly care and boost the country's female labour participation rate.[16]

Korean Elderly's Financial Vulnerabilities

The growing number of poor elderly has become an important social issue in South Korea. Several surveys have indicated that most elderly could not meet their daily expenses. According to the 2011 official survey, the average annual income for those aged above 65 was 8,496,000 KRW (about US$7,394). This is less than a third of the average annual income of a worker in SMEs. As mentioned in

---

[14] Data Source: Korean Statistical Information Service.

[15] "Youth Unemployment in Korea Reaches Highest in 15 Years", *The Korea Herald*, 26 July 2015, <http://www.koreaherald.com/view.php?ud=20150726000328> (accessed 20 April 2016).

[16] Lee Sang Ok and Tan Teck Boon, "South Korea's Demographic Dilemma", East Asia Forum, <http://www.eastasiaforum.org/2016/03/25/south-koreas-demo-graphic-dilemma/> (accessed 20 April 2016).

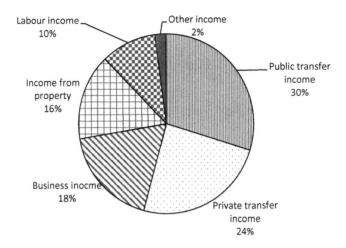

Figure 6-4   Source of Income for the Korean Elderly Aged above 65 in 2011
Source: Korean Statistical Information Service.

chapter 2, the monthly income for a worker in a company with 10–29 employees is US$2,172, an annual of US$26,064. As the elderly could not count on the support of the young, they have to depend on the government (a third of their income), followed by private fund transfer (24%), business income (18%), income from property (16%), labour income (10%) and other sources (2%) (Figure 6-4). The April 2015 official household survey showed that the household head aged 60 and above had the least income and spent more on food and health care than other younger households. Despite their relatively insignificant expenditure, they had little monthly surplus (Table 6-4). Living conditions for the elderly are hence difficult. As mentioned in chapter 5, the relative poverty rate for those aged 65 and older in South Korea stood at 48%, four times higher than the national average ratio (11.8%). The Gini coefficient for the elderly (0.42) is also higher than the country's average ratio (0.307).

As a result, debt to income ratio is high for this age cohort. A survey conducted by Korea Development Institute in 2015 revealed that people aged 60 and above in South Korea had the highest debt to income ratio (168%), much higher than the average debt ratio for all

Table 6-4   Household Monthly Income and Expenditure by Household Heads' Age in South Korea in April 2015

	30 Years Old and Below	40–49 Years Old	50–59 Years Old	60 Years Old and Older
Average age of household head	38	44	54	68
Number of household (persons)	3.35	3.67	3.10	2.45
A. Income (won)	4,176,959	4,886,823	4,992,232	2,978,118
B. Expenditure (won)	3,333,593	3,910,436	3,648,858	2,234,574
Distribution of expenditure (%)				
1. Food, alcoholic beverage and cigarette	**10**	**10**	**11**	**16**
2. Clothing and footwear	6	6	6	5
3. Housing, water, electricity, gas and other fuels	8	7	8	9
4. Household equipment and housekeeping services	4	3	3	4
5. Health	**5**	**4**	**5**	**9**
6. Transportation and communication	17	14	15	15
7. Entertainment, education, hotels and restaurants	21	27	19	14
8. Other consumption and non-consumption expenditures	28	29	34	28
C. Surplus (A-B)	843,366	976,387	1,343,374	743,544

Source: Korean Statistical Information Service.

other younger age cohorts (128%).[17] In 2015, 61% of Koreans between 55 and 79 years old were looking for jobs to meet their living expenses.[18] In the same year, 172,000 employees aged 60 or over were new hires, marking the fastest growth among all age groups according to Statistics Korea.[19]

The elderly's financial vulnerably could also be a result of changing social values. The Confucian tradition of younger generations taking care of their parents has been fading in South Korea. Official surveys indicated that more Koreans think that their parents should support themselves. According to the Asian Development Bank, familial transfers constitute about 45% of the lifecycle deficit for the elderly in Taiwan, 33% in Thailand but slightly under 20% for South Korea.[20] While traditional social value is changing in South Korea, the government is not able to quickly catch up with this newly developing trend. In 2011, the National Pension Scheme provided old-age pension benefits to only 28% of the elderly. In addition, the pension benefit was only 10% of the average income in the country.[21] If all types of pension (including public, private and basic pension) for the elderly are encompassed, 45% of the population aged between 55 and 70 would have benefited from the pensions in 2014 according to South Korea's official

---

[17] "Korean Elderly Carry Highest Debt Burden", *The Korea Times*, 18 November 2015, <http://www.koreatimes.co.kr/www/news/biz/2015/11/488_191273.html> (accessed 25 April 2016).

[18] "2015 Statistics on the Aged", Statistics Korea, <http://kostat.go.kr/portal/eng/pressReleases/11/1/index.board?bmode=read&bSeq=&aSeq=349205&pageNo=1&rowNum=10&navCount=10&currPg=&sTarget=title&sTxt=> (accessed 21 April 2016).

[19] "Rapid Population Aging Impacts South Korean Job Market", *Yonhap News*, 19 February 2016, <http://english.yonhapnews.co.kr/national/2016/02/18/65/0302000000AEN20160218000500320F.html> (accessed 20 April 2016).

[20] Lee Sang-Hyop and Andrew Mason, "The Economic Life Cycle and Support Systems in Asia", no. 283, October 2011, Asian Development Bank, p. 9.

[21] OECD Economic Surveys, Korea, June 2014, p. 29.

statistics.[22] Nonetheless, there is still 55% of the elderly aged between 55 and 70 (about six million people) who have no regular financial channels to finance their daily expenditures after retirement.

The financial difficulties are a frustration for senior citizens. The suicide rate among old South Koreans is by far the highest in the country and in the world. In 2013, the suicide rate in South Korea was 64.2 per 100,000 people for those aged 65 and older, significantly higher than the average suicide rate in the country (28.5 per 100,000 people).[23] The average suicide rate in OECD countries is 12 for every 100,000 population.[24] The 2014 official survey pointed out that economic difficulties were the principal reason for suicide (40.4%) of the elderly, followed by health reasons (24.4%), loneliness (13.3%), conflicts with family and friends (11.5%), family and friends' death, health problems and others (10.4%).[25]

Challenges for Financing the "Super-Aged" Society

South Korea's development had focused on economic growth rather than progress in social welfare spending. Along with the economic development, the country has gradually shifted its financial resources to social welfare in the recent years. As shown in Table 6-5, in 2013, health care and social contribution accounted for the largest share of South Korean government spending (37%), a big contrast to its tiny share in 1973 (8%). This growing expenditure on health care and social contribution led to a decline in the expenditure of other items such as

---

[22] "2015 Statistics on the Aged", Statistics Korea, <http://kostat.go.kr/portal/eng/pressReleases/11/1/index.board?bmode=read&bSeq=&aSeq=349205&pageNo=1&rowNum=10&navCount=10&currPg=&sTarget=title&sTxt= > (accessed 21 April 2016).

[23] "2015 Statistics on the Aged", Statistics Korea; Social indicator in 2014, Statistics Korea.

[24] "Korea's Suicide Rate Remains Top in OECD", *The Korea Herald*, 2 July 2014, <http://www.koreaherald.com/view.php?ud=20140702001045> (accessed 19 December 2014).

[25] Data source: Korean Statistical Information Service.

Table 6-5 Distribution of South Korean Government Spending 1973–2013

Unit: %

	Economic Affairs	Environmental Protection	Housing, Community Amenities, Recreation, Culture And Religion	Health and Social Contribution	Education	Defence and Public Order	Total Government Expenditure (billion KRW)
1973	34	2	7	8	25	24	855.7
1983	24	2	7	16	24	27	12,894.1
1993	26	4	8	22	21	19	59,052.8
2003	40	3	7	21	17	12	222,744.1
2013	20	3	6	37	20	13	372,580.5

Source: CEIC.

"economic affairs", which accounted for the largest share in 1973 (34%), but recorded a dip to 20% in 2013. The expenditure on "defence and public order" and education had also had a clear decline during the same period. In comparison, the shares of government spending on "environment protection", "housing, community amenities, recreation, culture and religion" have remained relatively unchanged.

The increased social spending, however, is still low compared to that of other OECD countries. In 2012, public social expenditure[26] accounted for 9.4% of South Korea's GDP, much lower than the average ratio of 20.9% in OECD countries (Table 6-6). In other aspects such as pension for senior citizens and survivors (2.5% of South Korea's GDP) and health-care services (4.1%), they were much lower than OECD countries' average of 7.9% and 6.2%, respectively (Table 6-6).

Given South Korea's relatively low debt to GDP ratio, it has more financial capacity for higher social welfare spending for the elderly than other countries. Its government debt to GDP ratio was 38% in 2014, much lower than the advanced economies' 110% and even lower than emerging market economies' 44%.[27] Nevertheless, as the number of the elderly is set to grow in the subsequent decades, the government's expenditure could become unsustainable in the long run. Hence, the tax burden on the young working population is expected to rise. The trend towards slowing economic growth and declining working population suggests that there will be less tax revenues to finance government spending. A tax spike on individuals would only discourage private consumption and investment. Private businesses may also relocate their companies overseas where the taxes are lower. South Korea is therefore facing a critical challenge when crafting policy responses to meet the enormous fiscal strains in the future.

Despite the visible challenges ahead, the country has not had a concrete plan to deal with this upcoming financial strain pertaining to the ageing demography. President Park Geun-hye had pledged to

---

[26] According to OECD, public social expenditure includes spending for old age, survivors, incapacity-related benefits, health, family, active labour market programmes, unemployment, housing and other social policy areas.

[27] *BIS Quarterly Review*, Bank for International Settlement, September 2015, p. 84.

Table 6-6   Breakdown of Public Social Expenditure as Percentage of GDP in 2012

As % of GDP

	South Korea	OECD
Cash benefits		
1. Pensions (for old age and survivors)	2.5	7.9
2. Income support for the working age population	1.1	4.4
Services		
3. Health	4.1	6.2
4. Other social services	1.7	2.4
Total public social expenditure	9.4	20.9

Source: OECD, Social Expenditure Database.

expand welfare benefits for the elderly and children "without raising taxes" before she was elected. However, since she took office in 2012, the welfare programme has been scaled down,[28] while more tax reduction to private business has been employed as a way to stimulate the economy. Notably, welfare policies were important battleground for political parties during the parliamentary election campaign in 2012 and 2016, even with the vague welfare programme proposals from both ruling and opposition parties. There is an urgent need to develop new approaches to meet the challenges of retirement and health-care services in the face of a greying society. The rising old age dependency burden could quickly translate into a potential government fiscal deficit crisis and dim economic development in the future.

Conclusion

South Korea's population structure has undergone tremendous transformation after WWII. The TFR declined from six children per woman in the early 1950s to 1.3 children per woman in 2015. Together with

---

[28] Chung Ah-young, "President's Welfare Policy Still Adrift", *The Korea Times*, 28 February 2016, <http://www.koreatimes.co.kr/www/news/nation/2016/02/116_199241.html> (accessed 26 April 2016).

rising life expectancy, senior citizens aged 60 and older is expected to account for over one-third of total population in 2030. Beyond the policy initiatives to constrain childbirth during the 1960s and 1980s, the high cost of living and education and other social factors following economic development (such as long working hours and longer period for education) have resulted in late marriages or a preference for a childless or one-child family. As a consequence, the share of senior workers in total domestic employment has increased whereas the share of young labour has dipped. The ageing demographic challenge could put the brakes on the country's economic development in the future.

The declining economic growth following the ageing demography can be seen from two aspects. First, consumption and investment are expected to fall as the aged has less consumption potential than the young. Second is the declining labour force. Female, youth and elderly's employment participation is likely to be promoted to make up for the shortfall in the shrinking young working population. South Korea will also need to largely increase productivity, particularly in services, in order to maintain the country's future economic prosperity. While immigrants could quickly fill the labour gap, it may not be a long-term solution given that immigrants would also age, and social integration and national identity issues could further complicate national development. Indeed, South Korea has the potential to boost its TFR given that most Koreans still believe in having children. According to a survey by the Hyundai Research Institute, 58% of adults want two children and 13.5% hope to have three. This is expected to raise South Korea's TFR from the current 1.3 to 1.8.[29]

There is also the advantage of a relatively low government debt to GDP ratio; South Korea is currently in a good financial position to stimulate the TFR. Nevertheless, promoting TFR is not only about providing childcare facilities and services. People's willingness and capacity to raise children is also contingent on the health of the

---

[29] "A Pram Too Far", *The Economist*, 26 October 2013, <http://www.economist.com/ news/special-report/21588207-faced-overwhelming-pressures-south-korean-women-have-gone-baby-strike-pram-too> (accessed 18 April 2016).

economic environment. South Korea needs a comprehensive development plan to provide public housing, control inflation, promote greater gender equality at the workplace, grant more subsidies to finance the growing household debt and so on. Although rules allowing flexible working days and paternity leave for fathers have been put into practice, many Koreans still think that childbearing is a mother's responsibility. The childrearing burden may discourage women's willingness to give birth. Social education to reshape perceptions about balance between family and work among men and women is thus essential.

Policy reforms that incorporate comprehensive social welfare provision and flexible employment are imperative in the face of a rapidly ageing population. In consideration of South Korea's particular government-business cooperative economic structure, the large companies will have an important role to play in tackling challenges to South Korea's rapid ageing demography. Large companies can take the lead in introducing flexible working days for married couples. The government and large businesses could also share costs through taxation relief and job creation for the married female, youth and senior citizens.

Conclusion

This book attempts to unravel South Korea's development after experiencing high speed economic growth rates during the Cold War era. The chapters with their different themes have discussions evolving around South Korea's major current economic concerns and potentially influential factors determining its economic prospects. The book also sheds light on different phases of its economic development and the policy responses that have been instituted. While this book seeks to use macroeconomic indicators and graphic descriptions to give an overall picture of South Korea's current economic situation, it also intends to contribute to the economic development literature. The discussions and investigations of this book will be useful reference for future work on comparative study of South Korea's contemporary and post-war development. A more comprehensive understanding of South Korea's economic development model can be established as a result.

Three issues are addressed and summarised in this concluding chapter. First, South Korea's export-led economy is challenged by the slowdown of US and European markets as well as China's quick industrial catching up. South Korea's economy is at a critical turning point for which a new growth model has yet to be found. Second, South Korea has expanded its FTAs network to sustain economic growth in this globalised world. The KORUS FTA and Korea-China FTA are representative of Korea's successful FTA expansion. The economic effect of FTAs remains to be seen. Third, the income inequality and ageing demography are the two emerging issues in South Korea's economy today. Policy initiatives have proven to be effective in improving income inequality. Nevertheless, the gap between the rich and the poor could still widen due to South Korea's greater involvement in the global economy. On the social front, South Korea has done little compared to developed countries in addressing its social welfare needs. The dramatic change in demography in the coming decade requires immediate remedial measures.

Whither South Korea's Next Engine of Growth?

The overreliance on exports of manufactured goods and on chaebols pose two main challenges to South Korea's economy. China's quick industrial catch up has also raised concerns about the sustainability of this growth model. The weak external demand from the West and the depreciation of the Japanese yen have further exposed the vulnerability of Korea's growth pattern. The waning exports have propelled the government to stimulate the economy through extra government spending. Nevertheless, as examined in Chapter 1, the economic growth rates fell far short of expectations despite the increased spending. Korea will need to make a shift from exporting intermediate goods to high technology-intensive products and providing high value-added services to the global market.

Although the more globalised production chain has been a boon for Korea's huge conglomerates' profitability and wages for their workers, Chapter 2 shows that these conglomerates provide employment to only a minority of domestic workers, leaving the less profitable SMEs to fill the country's employment gaps. South Korea's greater integration with the global economy has made ineffective the pro-business policies of the Lee Myung-bak and Park Geun-hye administrations. It is imperative for Korea to look for new growth engines to relieve its reliance on chaebols which enjoy certain distance from South Korea's economy and state's control. On the other hand, given chaebols' greater contribution to the country's production and exports, their presence is still needed especially in the country's efforts towards an innovation-based economy. While growth must be maintained at a decent level, the South Korean leadership will also need to work towards developing a mechanism that could support sectors and workers disadvantaged by the economic globalisation.

Balancing Korea's External Economic Relations

Diversifying South Korea's economic ties is considered one of the best strategies to sustain its long-term growth. The country's greater involvement in both bilateral and multilateral FTAs is to facilitate its economic expansion, open more markets for Korean exports and accelerate domestic economic reforms in line with those of advanced countries. Although it is inevitable that the less qualified workers and less competitive sectors at home would suffer from the economic opening up, the FTAs will make it more attractive for foreign investors who will make up for the limited job supply from chaebols. Likewise, Korean SMEs could seek to improve on their competitiveness and benefit from the "technology transfer" from foreign investors in the West. However, in spite of Korea's quick connection with the world through various FTAs, the efforts have yet to bear fruit.

In terms of trading partners, China and America are undoubtedly the most important countries in South Korea's external economic relations. China is Korea's most important overseas manufacturing site while the United States is a key consumption market for Korean manufacturers. The signing of FTAs with these two large economies has provided greater opportunities for Korean businesses to expand their goods and services. Korea's main competitors such as Taiwan and Japan have raised concerns as they have yet to sign FTAs with either China or the United States. With the FTAs, South Korea could have first-mover advantage in the Chinese and American markets. Chapter 3 shows that South Korea has witnessed a growing trade surplus in goods with the United States after the KORUS FTA was implemented. In particular, Korea's automobile trade surplus continued to progress despite its commitment to reduce tariffs for US automobile in its market. With China, the effect from the FTA may not be obvious in the short term owing to the slow implementation schedule. As addressed in Chapter 4, the slow opening in South Korea-China FTA could help reduce potentially huge damages to farmers and industries from the two countries. Beyond the economic considerations, the KORUS FTA is strategically important as it strengthens Korea's strategic alliance with the United States in view of the potential military threat from the North. The FTA with China is also of strategic importance for the advancement of their regional plans.

South Korea's Efforts Towards More Inclusive Economic Growth

Macroeconomic data from official statistics has been extensively employed to evaluate South Korea's development in this book. Nevertheless, the quantitative approach often reinforces outsiders' impression of "development" in terms of numbers, while ignoring the qualitative aspects such as sentiments, experiences and opinions of the locals. For example, the growing income inequality is one of the most important concerns in Korean society today; quantitatively, however, Korea's Gini index has been relatively encouraging vis-à-vis that of other countries in the world. As analysed in Chapter 5, the growing income inequality in South Korea can be attributed to the hollowing out of the manufacturing sectors, the limited employment created by profitable chaebols and labour market dualism. The domestic job opportunities cannot catch up with job losses from the relocation of manufacturing sectors to other countries. Chaebols' international business expansion benefited only a small number of its employees. The large number of layoffs and "labour flexibility" policy set by the International Monetary Fund after the Asian financial crisis has also caused an expansion of poorly paid non-regular workers with little social protection. Policy measures to tackle income inequality have been implemented. Indeed, income inequality requires not only long-term policy efforts but also strong societal consensus in support of these policies. In the short run, the country may continue to put more emphasis on stimulating economic growth if global economic growth prospects remain dim. The emphasis on economic growth may undermine the government's determination to equalise income distribution.

A more salient issue that could devastate Korea's economic growth prospects would be its ageing demography. As mentioned in Chapter 6, given its low birth rate, South Korea could become one of the oldest countries in the world in two decades. This development does not spell well for consumption and investment, and hence its economic growth. The shrinking young working population means that the country will have to rely on foreign workers, extend its retirement age, encourage female labour participation or increase labour productivity. The government will also have to increase welfare expenditure for the greater number of the elderly and boost the low birth rate. Overall, the trend towards slowing economic growth and declining working population suggests that there will be less tax revenue to finance government spending in the future. Strengthening the government's long term fiscal capability and devising a sustainable country-wide pension system are critical for the country's future development.

New Economic Development Strategy Needed to Deal with the Internal and External Uncertainties

When Park Geun-hye was elected in 2012, she had envisioned a "paradigm shift" for the economy driven by innovation and creativity, rather than by manufacturing production. In 2014, a three-year plan was proposed to restructure the economy by deregulating rules for service sectors' development and to boost domestic demand.[1] More than two years have passed, Park's "474 vision" (generating 4% economic growth, 70% employment rate and US$40,000 per capita income) through the three-year plan seems unlikely to be achieved. South Korea's economic growth rate is expected to reach 2.8% with

---

[1] "Park Aims for Overhaul of Economy with 474 Vision", *Korea Joongang Daily*, 26 February 2014, <http://koreajoongangdaily.joins.com/news/article/Article.aspx?aid=2985510> (accessed 15 November 2016).

US$25,989 GDP per capita and 63% of employment rate in 2016, lower than Park's initial target.[2] To minimise the impact from the slowing economy, the Special Act on Revitalising Companies or "One Shot Act" was passed in February 2016 to help the worst-affected industries in the economic slowdown. Tax breaks would be offered for firms that are selling their subsidiaries and rules for mergers and acquisitions relaxed.[3] Beyond the economic target that she failed to achieve, President Park also failed to attain "economic justice" as promised; chaebols' influence in the economy and state-business close relations continued. In November 2016, several chaebols, including Samsung, Lotte and SK have been raided by prosecutors in response to allegation of Choi's extortion of money for business licences or other benefits in return.[4] The impact of President Park Geun-hye's political scandal on the domestic economy has been constrained so far. It remains to be seen whether the strong opposition from society to chaebols' involvement in Park-Choi corruption cases will lead to weaker government-chaebols ties in developing the economy in the future.

Park's economic reforms fell through when the ruling party (Saenuri) lost its majority in the Legislative Election in April 2016. After the parliament voted for President Park's impeachment on

---

[2] Data source: International Monetary Fund and Korea Information Statistical Service.

[3] "South Korea's National Assembly Passes One Shot Act to Encourage Reorganization of Large Business, Corporate Governance", *JK Daily*, 6 February 2016, <http://www.jkdaily.com/articles/1813/20160206/south-korea-s-national-assembly-passes-one-shot-act-encourage.htm> (accessed 15 November 2016).

[4] Choi Soon-sil is the daughter of a South Korean Shamanistic-Evangelical cult leader, Choi Tae-min, an acquaintance of Park Chung-chee since the 1970s. Choi soon-sil and her father kept close relations with Park Geun-hye after Park Chung-hee was assassinated in 1979. In November 2016, Choi was officially charged by the prosecutors for intervening in state affairs and forcing chaebols to donate tens of millions of dollars to foundations and businesses she had control over. "Samsung, Lotte Heads Line up for Biggest Korean Corruption Probe", *The Business Times*, 5 December 2016, <http://www.businesstimes.com.sg/government-economy/samsung-lotte-heads-line-up-for-biggest-korean-corruption-probe> (accessed 5 December 2016).

9 December 2016, Saenuri has tried to disassociate itself from Park's political scandal to increase the chance of winning the presidential election in 2017. Park's unsuccessful economic reform means that South Korea's economy will continue to rely on exporting manufactured goods to sustain economic growth. However, as global growth is likely to falter,[5] Korean export prospect remains gloomy. "Brexit" and Donald Trump's election as US president further add uncertainties to the global economy. Trump plans to reduce US external trade deficits. South Korea is among the six countries[6] that America has large trade deficit with. Narrowing US trade deficit means Korea will have less foreign exchange reserves that could buffer a debt-triggered financial crisis. Trump also singled out South Korea-US FTA as a source of job loss in America during the election campaign. The fragile China-US relations after Trump's recent talk against China will add another uncertainty to Korea's economic outlook and regional prosperity. China plans to punish US automakers for their monopolistic behaviour,[7] while Trump had also stated his intention to impose tariffs of up to 45% on goods from China during the election campaign. How the tightly connected regional economies will be impacted from the China-US political and economic clash is a big question mark. From a positive point of view, Trump's pro-business policy may energise the US economy. The strong US dollar will also mean cheaper imported products for American consumers. With a stronger US economy, there is a likelihood that Korea could expand its exports to the US market. In the face of the internal and external uncertainties, South Korea is in urgent need of a new development strategy that could tackle all these potential changes.

---

[5] *Global Economic Prospect,* The World Bank, June 2016.

[6] The other five countries are China, Canada, Germany, Japan and Mexico. Peter Navarro, "Scoring the Trump Economic Plan: Trade, Regulatory and Energy Policy Impact", 29 September 2016, <https://assets.donaldjtrump.com/Trump_Economic_Plan.pdf > (accessed 5 December 2016).

[7] "Targeting US Automaker Signals Possible China Retaliation over Trump Talk", Reuters, 14 December 2016, <http://www.reuters.com/article/us-usa-trump-china-ramifications-analysi-idUSKBN1440AB?il=0> (accessed 15 December 2016).

Index

Printed in the United States
By Bookmasters